THE
FRIGATES

THE FRIGATES

An Account of the Lighter Warships
of the Napoleonic Wars
1793-1815

JAMES HENDERSON CBE

Drawings by Ernest E. Yelf

LEO COOPER
LONDON

First published in Great Britain by Allard Coles in 1970.
Published in this edition in 1994 by
LEO COOPER
190 Shaftesbury Avenue, London, WC2H 8JL

an imprint of Pen & Sword Books Ltd.,
47 Church Street, Barnsley, South Yorkshire, S70 2AS

A CIP catalogue record for this book is available from the British Library

ISBN 0-85052-432-6

Printed and bound in the USA

To Captain James Rowland, DSO and bar,
RN (retd) whose feats of warfare in command
of HMS *Wolverine* and her consorts in the
North Atlantic showed that the lights kindled
by the frigate captains still burn undiminished

Contents

Plates

The author is indebted to the Trustees of the National Maritime Museum, Greenwich for their kind permission to publish the plates reproduced in this book

Author's notes

A good deal of confusion often arises in reading early accounts of this period, due to the fact that so many ships were captured from the enemy and put into service under the same name. Thus at Trafalgar there were both an English and a French 'Swiftsure', an English and a French 'Neptune', with a Spanish 'Neptuno' to make it more difficult. To avoid all difficulty, the name of any ship under British command is printed in SMALL CAPITALS, while the ships of all other nations are printed in *italics*. At the moment a ship changes hands it changes typography. Thus there is no difficulty in knowing immediately under which command the BONNE-CITOYENNE was in May 1798.

An awkwardness often arises from the fact that many of the best early histories are compiled directly from the log of the ship engaged, an excellent method up to a point. The log noted the change of the year on 1st January, and the month on its first day but no other day; this was reasonable in a log which was intended to be read through, when submitted to Admiralty; but it can be intensely annoying when one reads, 'On the 21st., at 6 a.m., sighted a large sail, ENE about 8 leagues', and then has to turn back page after page to find out what month it was, and as many more to find out what year. I have therefore been particular in writing the full date unless obviously redundant.

The term 'starboard' has always been used for that side of the ship which is on your right as you face forward; at the time about which I write, and earlier, the other side was called 'larboard'. During most of the nineteenth century this was the name, but owing to the verbal difficulty of distinguishing larboard from starboard, it became customary to call larboard 'port'; this was easier, since not only was the port light red, but after dinner one passed the port to the left. However, I have retained 'larboard', because in print there is no confusion, and it corresponds with the contemporary accounts.

In helm orders one has to recall that all ships were steered by a tiller; in small ships this might appear on deck, and the sweep of deck-space required for the tiller was quite a serious tactical consideration. In larger ships the tiller was well below decks, perhaps twelve or fifteen feet long, operated by rope and tackle from the wheel on the quarter-deck, but still a tiller. Hence if one put the tiller over to starboard, the rudder and consequently the ship's head went round to larboard; therefore the helm order 'starboard' meant that the ship was to go to larboard. Much later, after steam and steam steering became almost universal, helm orders were changed by international agreement; the order 'port' meant 'turn to port' and the order 'starboard' meant 'turn to starboard'. I have retained the helm orders of the period, but have done what I can to avoid confusion.

The most important moment in an officer's career was his promotion to post captain; from this point on his seniority was assured. No other post captain could get ahead of him, however strong his 'interest'. At the same time, a lieutenant commanding a small ship, or promoted 'Commander' into a ship of less than post rank (twenty guns) was called 'Captain' so long as he was in command. To avoid confusion between an actual post captain, on the ladder which must inevitably lead him to flag rank if he survived long enough, and a junior officer in temporary command; I have used the substantive ranks of commander and lieutenant to indicate non-post captains, and 'Mr' to denote a warrant officer in temporary command. This is only of interest as regards ancillary ships, as a frigate could only be commanded by a post captain except in case of incapacity (wounds or death) in which case the lieutenants assumed command according to seniority. It was usual that after a meritorious action the first lieutenant of the British ship should be promoted commander, and given some ship of less than post force to show what he could do in actual command; thus gradually, as the war went on, was built the best cadre of naval officers that the world has ever seen.

It is a difficult point to determine how far a writer should interrupt himself to explain terms that are probably familiar to most of his readers. This I have dealt with by a fairly copious first chapter giving a sufficiently detailed general description of the frigates; an indexed sail plan (see endpapers) and a glossary. Thus the reader new to the period can inform himself as fully as he wishes, while those who know it well are not irritated by incessant explanations in the text.

Foreword

by Admiral of the Fleet
Sir Algernon Willis G.C.B., K.B.E., D.S.O., D.L.

This book by Mr James Henderson is particularly commended to those interested in the sea and in national defence.

In the 22 years of the Revolutionary and Napoleonic Wars (1793 to 1815) this country was engaged almost continuously in hostilities with France and, at times, with Spain, the Netherlands, and America as well. Our survival depended on supremacy at sea and this island produced a magnificent body of fighting seamen, who raised the efficiency of the British Navy to a state which has seldom been equalled. While the great victories over the enemy's battle fleets, such as St Vincent, the Nile and Trafalgar, gave us command of the sea, it was the smaller ships, notably the frigates, which exercised the control of sea communications enabling our trade to flow freely while cutting off most of that of the enemy.

These efforts led to countless frigate actions which our sailors fought with success, often against odds.

The graphic accounts of these actions and of other activities of the frigates related by Mr Henderson in this book make stirring reading, and take one back to the great days when, in the words of the younger Pitt: 'England saved herself by her exertions and Europe by her example.' Pitt, of course, intended to include the Scots, the Welsh and the Irish in this eulogy!

I wish this book the success it certainly deserves.

A. U. WILLIS
Petersfield   Admiral of the Fleet
Hampshire   August 1970

I

The Frigates

'Frigates!' cried Nelson, 'Were I to die this moment, *want of frigates* would be found engraved on my heart!' He was chasing round the Mediterranean in search of the French expedition to Egypt, the biggest overseas invasion ever mounted, with 75 warships, 400 transports, 10,000 sailors and 36,000 troops, horse, foot and artillery. Had Nelson had the four frigates which were originally detailed to join his squadron, he would inevitably have caught the expedition on the high seas and the whole of history would have been different; General Buonaparte would have ended his career, in all probability, in 1798 as a prisoner of war in England, or Naples if he were unlucky.

The term frigate appears to have originated in the Mediterranean, French *frégate*, Italian *fregatta*, and to have been at first applied to the galleass type of warship, about 250 tons, fitted with oars as well as sails. The first English ship to be called a frigate was the CONSTANT-WARWICK, about 380 tons, launched in 1646. According to Samuel Pepys, who was in a position to know, she was built on the lines of a captured Dunkirk privateer. The word came to be used rather loosely for any swift ship of some force, until the eighteenth century when the frigates came into the strict rating system of the Royal Navy. They were almost all fifth-raters, except for the small 28-gun class which were sixth-rate, which rate included anything down to a 20-gun post-ship, the smallest that could be commanded by a post captain. Smaller vessels were not rated, although well defined.

Because 'fifth-rate' sounds a long way down the list, many have thought that a frigate was a small ship of little force; but this was very far from the truth. Table I on page 169 gives a view of the rating system in 1794, when the 'ready' ships had been commissioned, and in 1814, before the run-down commenced. In this table, 'relegated' means out of commission and relegated to harbour or other duties; still useful, but not seagoing. Even VICTORY was relegated after the battle of Cape St Vincent, and served as a prison ship before being again commissioned as Nelson's flagship in the Mediterranean fleet.

The table shows at a glance that both at the beginning of the wars, and more especially at the end, by far the most numerous rates were the third rate, mostly 74-gun line-of-battle ships, and the fifth-rate frigates. The first and second rates, all three-deckers, were few in number, all fitted as flagships. In the third rate, the 64-gun ships were phased out as the war went on, and by 1814 there was only one in commission, the line being almost all 74s. The fourth-rate two-decker was a very small class, not fit to lie in the line of battle, unable to fight a ship of the line but too slow to get away. The fifth-rate 44-gun two-deckers were obsolete, having been built in 1744 to a design which even then was already obsolete. They were cranky, slow and unhandy, used mostly for convoy duties, and gradually relegated or broken up. The 28-gun sixth-rate frigates were gradually phased out during the period, so that at the height of the conflict the main strength of the Royal Navy was in the third-rate 74s and the fifth-rate frigates.

At a distance, hull down below the horizon, it was impossible to distinguish a frigate from a ship of the line; the difference in length was negligible, the sail plan was identical, and it was only when she came hull up that the higher sides and double row of ports showed the 74. Nevertheless, their roles were quite different. The 74 was built to carry as many and as heavy guns as possible, and to fight anything that floated. She was much higher, broader and deeper than the frigate, and consequently slower and less manoeuvrable. Battleships almost always operated in squadrons (less than ten ships) or fleets (more than ten); if a single one was detached, it was almost always because there was no frigate available.

The frigate, on the other hand, was not called upon to take on *anything*, only ships of her own class. From the battleship she was to stand away, and this she could do 'with ease and honour both', keeping well out of fighting range but having the enemy under constant observation, while she could fight any ship she could not avoid. Attached to a fleet, the frigates were the eyes and ears, ranging in line abreast over an immense expanse of sea while the battleships kept steadily on in line ahead, repeating signals and carrying despatches. In a fleet action, they assisted disabled ships and took possession of captured enemies. At that period, it was against the etiquette of war for a battleship to fire on a frigate during a fleet action, unless the frigate asked for it by firing first. Thus the frigate EURYALUS, Captain Blackwood, remained in the thick of the battle of Trafalgar, repeating signals first for Nelson and later for Collingwood, but sustained no damage or casualties, and was able to tow off the dismasted ROYAL SOVEREIGN. Detached either singly or in small squadrons, the frigates might be sent anywhere in the world to attack enemy commerce and protect their own, to hunt down privateers or pirates, or to take part in the conquest of yet another colony. The best voyage of all was to sail 'under Admiralty letter', that is, not under any senior officer but with direct instructions from Admiralty—usually sealed, to be opened at a stated latitude and longitude, so that no hint of destination might leak out before departure.

Quite surprisingly for a leading maritime nation, Britain produced no outstanding naval architect during the eighteenth century, and most of the frigates were built on the lines of captured French vessels, which were always superior in size and speed to their British counterparts. The *Danaé*, 941 tons, was captured in 1759 and from her were built the 36-gun 12-pounders of the beginning of our period. In 1782 the RAINBOW captured the *Hebé*, 1063 tons, 40 guns, and from her were built the earlier 36- and 38-gun frigates, 18-pounders. In April 1794 a frigate squadron under Sir John Borlase Warren captured the *Pomone*, 44 guns, 1239 tons, and she became the prototype of all the later heavy frigates.

In more than twenty years of warfare there were naturally changes in the ships engaged; a glance at Table II, page 170, will show the change from a majority of small and light frigates in 1794 to almost all large and powerful ships in 1814. Of frigates with a main battery of 12-pounder guns there were only 12 left in commission out of 68, while the 18-pounder classes had gone up from 20 to 113. The 40-gun 24-pounder class was taken from the lines of the *Pomone*, but the 44s had a different origin. When the *Pomone* was examined, it was realised that she had only been taken by the excellent handling of the British squadron, and that there was no frigate in the Royal Navy that could match her single-handed: how many more did the French have? Admiralty was beginning to have doubts about the 64-gun two-deckers, which were not really a match for the French 74s; three 64s were therefore cut down by having the whole of the upper deck removed, and the fore-castle and quarter-deck rebuilt on the main deck: retaining their powerful batteries of 24-pounders and the masts and rigging of 64s, they were real frigates for speed and handiness but were more than a match for any French frigate then afloat. They did notable service for many years, but were gradually phased out as they aged, and it was found that the new 38s and 36s could meet any French frigate afloat.

As these last two classes came to dominate the rating of frigate, I shall describe them in particular; the others differ merely in size and armament. A frigate was a long and fairly low ship, carrying its main battery of 18-pounders on a single deck, 14 or 13 ports each side according to whether she was a 38- or 36-gun frigate. Above this main deck the quarter-deck extended from the mainmast right to the stern, and the forecastle from the foremast to the bow. In both types the quarter-deck carried eight 9-pounder and the forecastle two 12-pounder long guns, plus four carronades on the quarter-deck and two on the forecastle, usually 24-pounders. The carronade was a very fair attempt to produce a short light gun which could nevertheless throw a heavy shot at comparatively short range, and many of the smaller ships of the Royal Navy were armed entirely with carronades; on the larger ships, however, frigates and 74s, the few carronades were generally reserved, loaded with two shot and a keg of musket-balls, to discourage any prospective boarding party on the opposing deck. Between the quarter-deck and the forecastle the bulwarks were carried well up, and deckbeams were laid over from side to side, just as if there were to be a complete second deck. On those beams, on each side of the ship, a gangway about six feet wide connected the two raised decks, and the larger boats and the spare spars were laid on the beams between the gangways.

Although there were a few experiments with other timbers when the ship-building programme was at its height, almost all the frigates were built entirely of oak, the main beams being at least a foot square in cross-section, and the planking four to five inches thick. This was proof against the musket-ball of the period, but cannon shot smashed through the planking and even the timbers, scattering deadly splinters all around, which caused far more casualties than shot. This was one of the reasons why officers opposed the use of teak, long after the Bombay-built ships had shown the superiority of teak for all maritime purposes: a splinter-wound from teak almost always goes septic, while an oak wound usually stays clean. The masts and spars were of pine, usually from the Baltic, and other timbers were used for particular purposes. All the frigates were extremely well built, fit to go to sea and stay at sea in any weather whatever. During the whole twenty-two years of war, only three frigates foundered at sea, and these were all very old ships, not really sea-worthy by frigate standards, and in each case it is clear that they met the centre of a tropical hurricane.

The frigates could carry six months' provisions, which meant that they could sail anywhere in the world without having to touch at any port. Full use was made of this mobility. In all the wide oceans of the world there was nowhere that the frigates were not sent, and nowhere that they did not find work to do. Well might Napoleon say bitterly, 'Wherever you find a fathom of water, there you will find the British.'

It has often been supposed that the frigates were very cramped for accommodation, as compared with the line-of-battle ships, but a simple comparison of known figures will show that it was quite the reverse. Take the favourite 38-gun 18-pounder which has been described: with a main deck about 150 feet long and 40 feet wide, and measuring at 1,060 tons, the whole complement was 277, officers, men and boys; very nearly four tons per man. No other class of warship had so much man-room. The 74 was usually about 1,700 tons, with a complement of 594—less than three tons per man. The big 112-gun first-rater, of 2,350 tons and a complement of 841, had just over 2¾ tons per man; and in addition had to provide the very considerable space required for an Admiral and his staff, who were not included in the ship's company. In the smaller ships, the 20-gun post-ship had about 3 tons per man, while the smallest were really packed. Of the brig SPEEDY, fourteen 4-pounders, 158 tons, Lord Cochrane, her commander, wrote, 'She was crowded, rather than manned, with a crew of eighty-four men and six officers, myself included.' This is 1¾ tons per man. It is therefore clear that the frigates had more tonnage per man than any other class, rated or not. The nearest modern comparison I can make is the now obsolete 'Admiralty V' class of destroyer, which served well in both great wars: 1,090 tons, complement 134. When one allows 425 tons for engines and boilers and 350 tons for fuel oil, it is clear that the balance of 'liveability' is all with the sailing frigate.

There was, of course, no pretence at equality in allocating this ample living space. Inequality was emphasised. The captain was not first, he was on a different plane altogether. Almost always a post captain of more than three years seniority, he wore a pair of epaulettes, which were worn only by the Marine officers in the rest of the complement. His accommodation was quite different from that of anybody else; under the quarter-deck, right aft, he had a dining-room, another day cabin, and two night cabins, even on the smallest 28-gun frigates. He had his own cook, steward, clerk and coxswain, who served nobody else. At the entrance to his quarters a Marine sentry was stationed night and day. When he appeared on the quarter-deck, the whole of the windward half was instantly cleared for his solitary promenade. Nobody dared to address him without permission. He might, once or even twice a week, invite his first lieutenant and one or two other officers to dine with him, and might include an occasional midshipman who had been recommended to him by some person of influence; but these were very formal occasions. Discipline had to be maintained, and maintained all the way; nobody thought very highly of a captain who was in the least familiar with his officers.

The only other commissioned officers on the ship were the lieutenants, usually four, and the two Marine officers. These were the commissioned officers of wardroom rank, to whom were added the sailing master, the surgeon, the purser, and the chaplain, if any; these were the warrant officers of ward-room rank, and could walk the quarter-deck, but their sleeping quarters were below, the surgeon and the chaplain near the cockpit, which was their action station, and the purser next his stores. The sailing master had a cabin below, but at sea he was hutched under the quarter-deck near the captain's quarters. The commissioned officers were housed in a row of cabins each not much more than a cube of six feet, all opening off the wardroom and fitted in, as best might, between the guns. All partitions were light and movable, for when the ship cleared for action the cabins and all their furnishings were thrown down into the hold. The wardroom officers had usually a common mess, to which everybody contributed equally, although there was nothing to stop anybody from opting out, either to live economically on the ship's rations or to indulge in private luxuries.

A deck below, the gunner presided in the gun-room over the senior warrant officers—boatswain and carpenter—and petty officers such as sailmaker, cook and armourer, master's mates and surgeon's mates, and also the very youngest boys in the ship, the 'captain's servants', young gentlemen not yet rated as midshipmen, although they could walk the quarter-deck, which the gun-room warrant officers could not. The midshipmen berthed in and around the cockpit, which became the surgery in action. Between the officers aft and the ratings forward were berthed all the lesser petty officers and also the Marines, about thirty of them, with a sergeant and three corporals. This was a precaution against nocturnal mutiny; the Marines were reckoned to be reliable under all circumstances.

Forward of the mainmast lived the ratings, a very mixed lot: professional warship sailors, very few, less than a sixth of the whole; fishermen and merchant sailors who had been conscripted by the press-gang—few ever volunteered; landsmen who had volunteered for the 'bounty', or to avoid gaol or debtor's prison, or to escape from difficult social circumstances. It was the business of the boatswain and his mates, under the first lieutenant, to make this mixed bag into a taut, close-knit ship's company, and usually they were successful.

Living was hard before the mast, but the hardships are often exaggerated by comparison with modern shore living;

by comparison with shore living, for the same class of people at that time, it was still hard but far from intolerable. Below decks the atmosphere was close and stuffy; but men whose blood is thoroughly oxygenated by a vigorous life in the open air invariably prefer a comfortable fug when they turn in. Hammock allowance was 14 inches per man, but of course as half were on watch this meant in effect 28 inches per man, 4 feet 8 inches per pair, a shade better than a double bed; and a clean hammock was infinitely superior to some straw on a damp floor. In a well-run ship great pains were taken to keep the ship and the men clean; vermin-borne diseases such as typhus which decimated armies on shore were very rare in the ships of the Royal Navy. Food was coarse and monotonous, but few had ever had much better, and at least they were sure where the next meal was going to come from. Drink was only too plentiful. The allowance of beer was a gallon a day, and of rum half a pint; but this rum was almost pure alcohol, and when cut down, as it was, with two pints of water it was still equivalent to very nearly two bottles of rum at the strength at which it is retailed today. Anybody today who drank eight pints of beer and the best part of two bottles of spirits every day would be put down as an alcoholic, yet this was the daily ration for every man in the Navy. It was eagerly expected. The severest punishment less than flogging was to cut a man's rum ration off for a week; the withdrawal symptoms must have been very unpleasant, but no doubt a popular type would get 'sippers' from his mess-mates. To be drunk was a serious naval crime, but many men must have been at least tipsy every afternoon. Far more men lost their lives through drink than by enemy action, and lunacy was all too common, mostly from frequent head injuries caused by running against overhead beams while drunk. Admiral Lord Keith considered that almost every crime, and the majority of casualties, were caused by excessive rum; yet he dared not suggest to cut the ration. Did not Solomon advise, 'Let him drink, and forget his poverty, and remember his misery no more.'

To understand the importance of sea-borne cannon, it is necessary to compare with land guns. At that time, the standard field-piece was a 6-pounder, and owing to difficulties of transport they were few; even at Waterloo Wellington could deploy only 156 guns of assorted nationalities. The twenty-eight 18-pounders of the 38-gun frigate would on land form the siege train for the assault of some major fortress, hauled up by hundreds of animals at a few miles a day; but the frigate, under favourable conditions, could carry her formidable battery two hundred miles in the twenty-four hours. The 18-pounder was nine feet long, weighed two tons, and required ten men to handle it. On firing, the force of the recoil sent it running inboard on its carriage to the full length of the breeching-tackle which secured it to the ship's side; it was then sponged out with a swab, the powder in its cloth cartridge rammed down with a wad on top, then the shot and another wad; the cloth of the cartridge was pierced and a little fine priming-powder poured into the touch-hole. The gun-crew then ran the gun out by heaving on the breeching-tackle, after which the gun-captain adjusted his aim. The modern guns were fired by flint-lock and lanyard, but slow-match was always kept ready in case of emergency. The management of the gun was heavy work, especially in rough weather. Under good conditions with a well-trained crew, a shot every two minutes was a very good rate of fire.

While during the twenty-two years of the wars Britain was at some time or other in conflict with every maritime Power except Portugal, it was, of course, the French who were the most frequent antagonists, and the most carefully studied by British officers. For equivalent gun-power, the French frigates were larger, better designed, and more numerously manned (up to a hundred more) than their British counterparts. In tactics, the desire on either side was to get athwart the enemy's stern, where the whole broadside could rake the whole length of the ship with only two or four guns able to reply; but usually it came to a mutual cannonade at about fifty yards range. The British fired low, on the downward roll of the ship; the French fired high at the rigging, on the upward roll. The British idea was to kill the crew and dismount the guns; the French wished to disable the sailing power of their enemy, hoping to be able to take a favourable position for cannonade, musketry or boarding with their superior numbers. The British tactics were much more effective; in almost every action the French casualties were much heavier than the British, and the French usually lost. During the period 1793 to 1815, the British lost 17 frigates to the French, of which 9 were recaptured; whereas

1 The Palisades. 2 Fort Charles. 3 Port Royal, Headquarters, C-in-C, West Indies Station. 4 Apostles Battery. 5 Port Henderson. 6 Fort Augusta. 7 Passage Fort. 8 Town of Kingston. 9 Military Camp. 10 Fort Nugent. 11 Gallows Point. 12 Kingston Harbour. 13 Harbour Head. 14 Passage into the Harbour through the reefs.

in the same period the French lost 229 frigates to the British. Very few were sunk; it is very difficult to sink a wooden ship by above-water bombardment: the accepted form was that when a ship had sustained such damage and losses that she could not continue the action with any hope of success, she should haul down her flag and surrender.

Engaging in war has always an element of risk, so has going to sea, and in those days especially so had going to a tropical climate. Those not closely acquainted with the period may be surprised that of these three hazards climate was the chief, sea-going next, and combat almost negligible. Taking the whole of the wars, more than half the deaths were by disease, chiefly tropical. Scurvy was still a danger, though not so fearful as in 1740, when Anson lost by scurvy two-thirds of the complement of his squadron between Britain and Juan Fernandez. For the rest, about forty per cent of all deaths were from the hazards of the sea—shipwreck, fire, explosion, falling from rigging, and personal accidents, mostly when drunk. In the whole Royal Navy during the whole period, less than ten per cent of the deaths were in action; and in frigates, which were not required to take part in the great fleet encounters, deaths in action cannot have been more than five per cent of the total death-roll. In a frigate duel, on the British side ten killed and twenty wounded was a pretty heavy casualty list.

The mosquito was far deadlier than the French cannon. Most histories ignore or play down the incidence of disease, and play up the great battles; but it is all the same to a widow's husband whether he meets a cannon-ball in an action or dies in a stinking hospital in the Caribbean; and the latter was at least ten times more likely. During only two years of operations in the West Indies, the army lost by 'Yellow Jack' twenty times as many British soldiers as were killed at Waterloo. The British seamen were not supplied with statistics, but they were perfectly well aware of how many of their shipmates they had seen more or less buried at the Palisades* compared with the number they had seen killed in action. Given good officers, they looked forward eagerly to battle, not only with the natural zest of warriors, but with the hope of gain; prize money might very well set up a man for life in his sphere of society. Under any good captain they engaged with every confidence: under a great captain—and at least fifty of the frigate captains were born leaders of men—they went into action in the highest spirits, each man sure of his comrades, each determined to do his duty and absolutely confident of victory.

* The Palisades was a beach at Jamaica, where the dead from the hospitals were buried in very shallow graves in the sand. The land crabs completed the disposal. This Aceldana is now the airport.

2

Success Story

When the French National Convention declared war on Britain on 1st February 1793, it took some time to get the great battle fleets to sea. Of the ships already in full commission, squadrons had to be sent to distant stations to carry the news and to assemble the merchants into convoys, protect their own and harass the enemy. The British stores had been so well assembled by the Comptroller of the Navy, Sir Charles Middleton, volunteers came in so readily and the press-gang was so busy, that by July the number of line-of-battle ships in full commission had been increased from 26 to 54, and the Royal Navy could put out powerful fleets into the Mediterranean and the Channel, as well as meeting its distant commitments in India and the West Atlantic. Almost immediately on the declaration of war, however, there sailed from the ports on both sides of the Channel swarms of small vessels, both of the regular navies and of privateers, all anxious to snap up some richly-laden merchantman of the other side who had not yet heard of the war.

A privateer was a ship owned and fitted out by private persons, who received 'letters of marque' from a sovereign power; these entitled them to carry on war at their own risk and expense, and for their private profit, and at the same time ensured that if captured, the crews were to be treated as prisoners of war. It was in effect licensed piracy, and in fact many known pirates, especially in the West Indies, applied for and received letters of marque, thus legalising their trade so long as they confined it to the ships of the enemy. Many British privateers were fitted out, but as the war continued and the grip of the British blockade tightened and the French overseas colonies were captured, British privateering practically disappeared, simply because it was no longer profitable. French merchantmen were so scarce, so well armed and so well escorted, that the distant profit just wasn't worth the certain expense and probable risk. The French privateers, on the other hand, were a thorn in the side of the British marine during the whole of the wars. Built for the purpose, well armed, and manned by the bold and experienced mariners of Brittany, they could run from any ship of war and over-awe almost any merchantman except the heavily-armed ships of the Honourable East India Company. Immediately on the outbreak, the small warships of both Navies, brigs, sloops, and a few frigates, were sent into the Channel and its approaches, to look for enemy ships and of course snap up what prizes they could.

In May 1793 the frigates VENUS and NYMPHE left Falmouth on a cruise in the Western Approaches, and finding little of interest, they separated to cover a wider field. Early in the morning of the 27th May the VENUS, about 300 miles west of Cape Finisterre, came across the *Semillante*, a frigate of about twenty-five per cent more force; a sharp action ensued, of which the *Semillante* had much the worse; but just as the VENUS was closing in for the kill there hove in sight the *Semillante*'s consort, the *Cléopâtre*, a fresh and powerful frigate, and the VENUS could only run as well as her damaged rigging would permit. The *Cléopâtre* chased her for two days, until she was rejoined by the NYMPHE, when the *Cléopâtre* in turn made off. Both the French ships went into Cherbourg, then quite a small port, while the British pair made Falmouth.

The NYMPHE was a frigate of the 36-gun class, 938 tons, mounting twenty-six long 12-pounders on the main gun-deck, with two long 6-pounders and eight carronades, 24-pounders, on the quarter-deck and forecastle, and with a total complement of 240 officers and men. She was commanded by Captain Edward Pellew, a Cornishman who had already been favourably noticed for seamanship, knowledge of the dangerous French coast, and capacity for training a crew. The VENUS being under repair, Pellew left Falmouth on the 17th of June, 1793, to cruise in the Channel, with some hope that the *Cléopâtre* might be doing the same, she being, as far as was known, the only French ship of force north of Brest; the *Semillante* was safe enough for a few months.

Once, in the Roman Senate, a Commander-in-Chief was chosen on the grounds that in addition to all his military virtues 'He is favoured by Fortune'. Thus it was with Pellew: he was always lucky. Early the very next morning, about twenty miles south of Start Point, a large sail was observed to the south-east, and this was none other than the *Cléopâtre*. She was of almost exactly the same force as the NYMPHE, but with eighty more men in her crew. At first she bore away, and both ships continued under full sail in a fair breeze on that fine June morning. The NYMPHE was overtaking, and when Captain Mullon of the *Cléopâtre* recognised her, he shortened sail and cleared for action until the NYMPHE came up with her about six o'clock. A curious ceremony now took place, reminiscent of an earlier generation; of course the war was yet young, and very few in either ship had ever been in action. As the ships closed, the captains hailed each other and saluted by taking off their hats; the crew of the NYMPHE shouted 'Long live King George' and gave three cheers, led by the captain waving his hat from the quarter-deck. Captain Mullon waved a cap of liberty to his men, who shouted 'Vive la République', and nailed the cap to the mast-head. Then, as the guns came to bear, Captain Pellew put on his hat and the NYMPHE's broadside thundered out. The *Cléopâtre* answered immediately, and at little more than a ship's length apart a furious cannonade carried on for three-quarters of an hour, the raw crews serving their guns like veterans, the captains gravely walking the quarter-decks amid the storm of shot. Suddenly, at the same time, both the mizzen-mast and the steering wheel of the *Cléopâtre* were shot away, and, out of control, she swung around head-on to the NYMPHE, her jib-boom passing between the fore and main masts of her opponent. She kept on swinging, until the jib-boom was pressed so hard against the mainmast of the NYMPHE that it looked as if it would carry away the damaged mast; but the jib-boom broke. The two ships remained hooked together by the rigging, and Captain Pellew, thinking that the enemy intended to board him with their superior numbers, ordered his own boarders up to repel them. However, the *Cléopâtre* was in no condition for boarding, all her commissioned officers having been killed or wounded, and seeing some sign of confusion, Captain Pellew instantly gave the order to board. His men leapt over the bulwarks on to the forecastle of the *Cléopâtre*, and through the gun-ports on to her main deck. With a fierce rush along the deck and the gangways they reached the quarter-deck, and in less than ten minutes hauled down her colours.

On the quarter-deck they found the heroic Captain Mullon mortally wounded, his left hip and part of his back having been carried away by a round-shot. Resolute in his duty to the last, he remembered that he had in his pocket a list of private coast-signals, and as he lay in his death-throes he pulled a paper from his pocket, bit it to pieces and was trying to swallow it when he died. In fact the paper he destroyed was his Captain's commission, and the signals fell into British hands; but no mistake could dim his heroic devotion to duty.

In so close and fierce an action, it was to be expected that casualties would be heavy. The NYMPHE had 23 killed, including 5 warrant officers, and 27 wounded, including 2 lieutenants and 2 midshipmen. The *Cléopâtre* had 63 killed and wounded, including her captain killed and all 3 lieutenants wounded. Both ships were extensively damaged, but repairable, and both arrived at Portsmouth on the 21st.

As has been said, Pellew was always lucky. This was the very first naval battle of the war which was fought out to a finish between ships of equal force manned with equal courage and resolution, and the result was a decisive British victory, with the captured vessel brought into a British port. King George III came down in person to Portsmouth and knighted Captain Pellew, the first hero-knighthood of the wars. His brother, Commander Israel Pellew, had been with him as a volunteer, having no ship at the time, and the King of his own authority made him a post captain. First-Lieutenant Amherst Morris was promoted Commander by Admiralty, which also bought in the prize, changing the name to OISEAU as there was already a CLEOPATRA in the Royal Navy. A tidy bit of prize-money nicely rounded off the honours.

Captain Israel Pellew was perhaps unlucky in that he spent the whole of his naval career under the shadow—the beneficent shadow—of his elder brother. He had a satisfactory career, ending up a knight and an admiral, but he was always being compared with his big brother. Israel commanded the CONQUEROR at Trafalgar, and early in the battle took possession of the French flag-ship, the *Bucentaure*. He sent his Captain of Marines on board to arrange the formalities of the surrender of the Commander-in-Chief, Vice-Admiral Villeneuve, who asked to what ship he had surrendered. 'The CONQUEROR, Captain Pellew.' 'Ah, I am happier to know that I have to give my sword to so distinguished an officer as Captain Sir Edward Pellew.' Perhaps Israel was a better name for a patriarch than for a captain; perhaps he was just not so lucky. His first frigate command, the AMPHION, was lying in harbour at Plymouth on 22nd September 1796 when she took fire and blew up, killing most of the crew and their visitors from shore.

Sir Edward Pellew was now given the 38-gun frigate ARETHUSA, while the NYMPHE, after repairs, was commanded by Captain George Murray. In the spring of 1794 they formed part of a squadron of five frigates cruising off the Breton coast, under the command of Commodore Sir John Borlase Warren in the FLORA, the others being the MELAMPUS, Captain Thomas Wells, and CONCORDE, Captain Sir John Richard Strachan. On the 23rd of April, before dawn, they descried a strange squadron, which turned out to be the French frigates *Engageante*, *Resolue* and *Pomone*, with the corvette *Babet*, standing in line ahead in that order. The *Babet* was out of her class, having only twenty 8-pounders and two brass 6s. The FLORA overtook the *Babet* at 6.30 a.m, and firing into her, passed ahead and engaged the *Pomone*, a very different proposition, being the most powerful frigate in the world at that time. The ARETHUSA, next ahead, now engaged the *Babet*, which surrendered at 8.30 a.m., after a most courageous resistance to very superior force. By this time the FLORA had had such a hammering from the *Pomone* that she had to drop astern, and now stopped to take possession of the *Babet* while the ARETHUSA and CONCORDE pushed on to overtake the *Pomone*, which had also been much damaged by the fire of the FLORA. Under the cannonade of the two British frigates, both her main and mizzen masts crashed down, and the shattered spars took fire; thus crippled, she hauled down her colours at 9.30 a.m., and was taken over by the ARETHUSA.

The Commodore now signalled the CONCORDE and MELAMPUS to chase the remaining two frigates, the NYMPHE being too far in the rear to have much hope of catching up. The CON-CORDE, being the better sailer, intended to engage the *Engage-ante* in passing, hoping to do her enough damage to slow her down until the MELAMPUS could come up. However, the *Resolue* came to the aid of her consort, and together they did so much damage to the CONCORDE's rigging that she was glad to hang back and refit. The *Resolue* now stood ahead, and Sir Richard Strachan decided to make sure of the *Engageante* and let the other go. The battle lasted until 1.45 p.m., when the French frigate, having been so knocked about that she could neither fight nor flee, at last surrendered.

The British squadron was so superior in force that the result was to be expected: the great interest was the capture of the *Pomone*. Admiralty was surprised at her size and force; it had not been thought in the least likely that the Revolutionary Government could so quickly produce an entirely new and superior class of warship, and steps had to be taken to cope, as already described (p. 4). The *Pomone* was taken into the Royal Navy, and later became for a time the flagship of Sir John Borlase Warren; the *Engageante* was too much battered to go to sea, and became a hospital ship; the *Babet* was added to the Royal Navy as a sloop, but was lost in 1801 with all hands, in a West Indian hurricane.

Sir John's squadron continued to make things difficult off all the coast of Brittany, especially in the vicinity of Brest, where a formidable French fleet was gathering. On the 23rd August 1794 they attacked a French frigate and two corvettes, and drove them on to the rock-bound shore. The squadron was becoming the theme of the ballad-mongers—

> *'If they run, why we'll follow, and run them ashore,*
> *And if they won't fight us, what can we do more?'*

The ARETHUSA had a good name for balladry, lucky again:

> *'Come all ye jolly sailors bold,*
> *Whose hearts are cast in honour's mould,*
> *While English glory I unfold,*
> *Huzza for the* ARETHUSA!'

On the 21st October 1794 Sir Edward Pellew in the ARETHUSA found himself in command of a small squadron: ARTOIS, Captain Edmund Nagle, DIAMOND, Sir William Sidney Smith, and

GALATEA, Captain Richard Goodwin Keats. It is striking how many of the frigate captains of those early days became famous admirals before the wars ended; of course at that time ships were scarce, and Admiralty could give each one a picked captain and a picked crew too. On this day they sighted a big French frigate and gave chase; the ARTOIS sailed so much better than the others that she was alone when she overhauled the *Revolutionnaire*. Action lasted less than three-quarters of an hour, when the French crew refused to fight any more and forced the captain to surrender after a loss of eight killed and four wounded, as against three killed and five wounded in the ARTOIS. While the French ship was definitely more powerful than the British, she was on her first cruise. Being little damaged, she was a valuable addition to the Royal Navy, and Captain Nagle was knighted.*

What with captures and what with building, more ships were becoming available, and for the 1796 campaign there were two powerful frigate squadrons to cruise the waters around Brest, one under Sir John Borlase Warren in the POMONE, and the other under Sir Edward Pellew in the INDEFATIGABLE, one of the new 44-gun frigates made by taking a deck out of a 64-gun ship of the line. In his squadron was the recently captured REVOLUTIONNAIRE, Captain Francis Cole. The squadron sighted a French frigate, and Pellew ordered Cole to get between her and the land, being a few miles off Ushant. This Captain Cole was able to do, but the night falling misty, he lost sight of her until after 9 p.m., when he made all sail and chased at great speed, coming up with her about midnight. Captain Cole hailed the French frigate, inviting her to surrender without fighting, in view of the powerful squadron coming up; this the French captain refused, but after a couple of broadsides the crew called out that they had surrendered. The ship was the *Unité*, Captain Durand-Linois, of considerably less force than the REVOLUTIONNAIRE, and having had nine killed and eleven wounded, while the British had no casualties at all. The fact that both the *Revolutionnaire* and the *Unité* were surrendered by their crews against the wishes of their officers shows that the French Navy had not yet recovered from the anarchy of the Revolution. The

* The ARTOIS, Captain Sir Edmund Nagle, wrecked on the French coast, 31st July 1797.

1 *Droits de l'homme* engaged by INDEFATIGABLE: AMAZON coming up

2 AMBUSCADE boarded and captured by *Bayonnaise*

3 SAN FIORENZE and *Piémontaise*

4 FISGARD and *Immortalité*

5 Boats of the SURPRISE cutting out the *Hermione*

6 SYBILLE taking the *Forte*

7 Basque Roads. IMPERIEUSE leading in

8 IMPERIEUSE and *Calcutta*

surrender did not affect the career of Captain Linois, as we find him later as a Rear-Admiral commanding a squadron in the Indian Ocean. In this case, as well as having a mutinous crew, he was handicapped by the presence on board of the wife of the Governor of Rochefort with a large family and domestic staff; Captain Pellew stopped a neutral merchant ship and put the family and retainers on board to continue their journey.

On the 20th of the same month, when the squadron was returning to Plymouth, a strange sail was sighted and the recognition signal was not replied; Pellew went in chase along with the AMAZON and CONCORDE. The chase went on for fifteen hours at high speed, 168 miles being run at an average of 11 knots; the INDEFATIGABLE was well ahead of her consorts, and brought the enemy to action about midnight. The fight continued under full sail for two hours, during which time the French ship lost her mizzen-mast and main top-mast, and the INDEFATIGABLE lost her gaff and her mizzen top-mast. The action was broken off while both made what repairs they could to their rigging, when the AMAZON and CONCORDE came up, and after they had taken up good positions the French ship surrendered. She was the *Virginie*, Captain Bergeret, who was highly praised by Sir Edward in his official despatch, having had fifteen killed and twenty-seven wounded, and four feet of water in the hold, before he surrendered to an overwhelming force. The INDEFATIGABLE had no casualties whatever. The *Virginie* was a very fine new frigate of over 1,000 tons, and after repair was a most acceptable addition to the Royal Navy.

Aggression was the keynote of the policy of the French Directorate; *l'attaque, l'attaque, et toujours l'attaque*. Indeed, this policy had won them astounding victories over all Europe, and had battered most of western Europe into either submission or alliance. Of the maritime nations, Holland declared war on Britain in May, Spain in October of 1795. The combined fleets far out-numbered the British, who also could not abandon their far-spread responsibilities. The Directorate planned an attack on British soil; in the summer of 1796 General Hoche had a conference at Basle in Switzerland with Arthur O'Connor and Lord Edward Fitzgerald, the Irish patriots or traitors, depending on the angle of view, when a plan for a major invasion of Ireland was roughed out, and Wolfe Tone came to France to assist in the preparations and action. The French had contemplated landing 25,000 troops; the Irishmen thought 15,000 was enough (neither of the delegates had ever seen an army assembled) and were able to assure the French (who had no experience of negotiating with Irishmen) that immediately a French army landed it would be joined by a quarter of a million armed patriots. Their own imagination fired, the Directorate thought up a two-fold plan: the French Navy, having landed the Army in Ireland, was forthwith to proceed to India and conquer the British empire there; however, sanity broke through, and it was decided that the conquest of Ireland would be enough for one campaign. The plan was well worked out; the disembarkation was to be in Bantry Bay, and three different landing places were selected, according to the wind which might be blowing at the time; if none was feasible, then the troops were to debark at the mouth of the Shannon; should the fleet scatter during the approach, the ships were to rendezvous off Mizzen Head and remain thereabouts for five days to gather again. The only things left out of the calculations were the Royal Navy and the weather; as things turned out, the Channel Fleet was absent, and the job had to be done by Admirals December and January, plus a few frigates.

By November, General Hoche and Vice-Admiral Morard-de-Galles had everything in readiness at Brest, awaiting only two reinforcing squadrons; one, under Rear-Admiral Richery, did not arrive until 11th December, and the Toulon squadron under Rear-Admiral Villeneuve (he who lost at Trafalgar nine years later) did not seem to be coming at all. It was decided to set out, and on the 15th December the great fleet moved out of harbour and anchored in Camaret Bay; there were 17 line-of-battle ships, 13 frigates, 6 corvettes, 7 transports and a partially disarmed frigate serving as a powder transport. In addition to the large crews, the fleet had on board an army of probably 18,000 men, horse, foot and artillery, with vast quantities of stores; thus encumbered, they were to face the Royal Navy and the Atlantic in mid-winter.

The main Channel Fleet, under Lord Bridport, had gone into Portsmouth for the winter, agreeable to Admiralty instructions, leaving off Brest a strong squadron of line-of-battle ships under Vice-Admiral Colpoys, cruising about forty miles offshore, with an inshore squadron under Captain Sir Edward Pellew in the INDEFATIGABLE, having under his command the REVOLUTIONNAIRE, Captain Francis Cole, the AMAZON, Captain Robert Reynolds, the PHOEBE, Captain Robert Barlow, and a small armed lugger the DUKE OF YORK, Mr Sparrow. Immediately on observing the decisive movement of the French fleet, Sir Edward despatched the PHOEBE to inform Colpoys and, probably having doubts as to the promptitude of that very senior officer, at the same time sent the AMAZON to Portsmouth.

The French fleet had intended to sail out by the passage d'Iroise, the direct route from the port, but seeing the frigates so bold about the entrance, the Vice-Admiral concluded that they must be strongly supported, and he would run the risk of his ships being destroyed in detail as they came forth; so, the wind being fair from the east, he decided to take the southward passage through the dangerous Raz de Sein. Darkness falling and the wind rising gusty, he changed his mind and made for the passage d'Iroise, followed by those of the fleet who could divine his intentions. As a guide, he stationed a corvette at a suitable spot, with directions to fire guns, rockets and blue-lights to keep the fleet on the right track. Pellew thought he would like to join in the fun, so he took the INDEFATIGABLE right in among the French fleet, where he too fired guns, rockets and blue-lights, greatly to his own pleasure and the confusion of the French, so much so that the 74-gun *Seduisant* went ashore on the Grand Stevenet rock near the entrance of the Raz; here she too, as signals of distress, began to fire guns, rockets and blue-lights, to add to the general mayhem. During the night she became a total loss, with more than half her complement of 1,300 men.

Having satisfied himself that the whole fleet had put to sea, and, in the prevailing easterly wind, could not get back into harbour, Pellew sent the REVOLUTIONNAIRE with this information to Vice-Admiral Colpoys, and his little lugger to Falmouth with the same news. Later in the same day, having completed his job of watching the enemy and reporting their movements, he decided that he would not do much good hanging about there and went off to Falmouth himself, arriving on the 20th December and reporting to Admiralty by the semaphore telegraph.

Meanwhile the French fleet had got fairly to sea, but in

three separate detachments, out of sight of each other and, fortunately for them, out of sight of Colpoys' fleet of thirteen ships of the line; and also out of sight of their leaders, who had, for reasons doubtless clear to themselves, embarked together in the fast frigate *Fraternité*. Colpoys was somewhat at a loss, but on the 20th sighted a squadron of French line-of-battle ships and gave chase; this, however, was the tardy reinforcement from Toulon, which in the dirty weather got clean away and went into L'Orient. In the chase and the weather the British fleet was damaged and scattered, and Vice-Admiral Colpoys turned up at Spithead on the 31st with only six ships left under his command.

Somehow the fragments of the French fleet met at the rendezvous off Mizzen Head in a spell of fine weather on the 21st, lacking only the *Seduisant*, wrecked, and missing the *Nestor*, 74, the *Fraternité*, frigate, with the two commanders-in-chief, and two other frigates. Rear-Admiral Bouvet, an excellent sailor, took command of the ships, and General Grouchy (who did *not* distinguish himself at Waterloo eighteen years later) took over the Army; but try what they could, they could not get up Bantry Bay. Christmas Day, when Lord Bridport was trying to get the Channel Fleet out of Spithead, was the coldest in living memory; indeed, the coldest since 1708; moreover, a bitter east wind drove a thin snow along with it. Now the French could appreciate the sailing directions given to the Great Armada two centuries before: 'Take great heed lest you fall on the island of Ireland, for fear of the harm that may befall you on that coast, where the ocean sea raiseth such a billow as can hardly be endured by the greatest ships.' Some went ashore, some collided with each other; all the survivors were blown out of the Bay, and eventually, despairing of success and short of provisions, they made the best of their separate ways back to France, harried by six frigates out of Cork.

One of the last to leave the coast was the *Droits de l'Homme*, 74, Commodore la Crosse, a very good officer, having also on board the famous General Humbert. Pursuant to orders, the Commodore went to the second rendezvous, the mouth of the Shannon, where he captured a small British privateer and took her crew and passengers on board as prisoners. On the 7th January, as nobody else appeared, he left the station and made for France, intending to make a landfall on Belle Isle and then go into one of the harbours in that vicinity. On the 13th January he thought himself in the correct latitude and about seventy or eighty miles west of his objective, the weather coming up foul from the westward. He sighted through the mist and rain two large ships to windward, turned away, and was glad to lose sight of them: actually they were French. Two hours later, with the storm rising and the sea very rough, the *Droits de l'Homme* descried two more ships to leeward, between her and the land, wherever that might be; and what ships were these but the INDEFATIGABLE and the AMAZON, back on station!

Commodore la Crosse was a brave and experienced seaman, and knew very well what an immense superiority a ship of the line had over two frigates, even if one was larger than usual; but he also had on board a valuable battalion of soldiers, many of whom must inevitably be killed in a gunnery battle, and also an important General. The wind was rising, and backing to south-west, a bad sign; and just after he sighted the British frigates a sudden squall carried away both his main and fore top-masts, cumbering his decks with wreckage and reducing his power of manœuvring. This made up his mind, and after clearing the fallen spars he set off before the wind to the eastward, under mainsails only.

Sir Edward Pellew was no swashbuckler, to rush into battle regardless of any consideration; he knew the rule that frigates did not engage line-of-battle ships, and also that if he did engage and lost his ship he would be in serious trouble for hazarding her against odds which all experience showed to be impossible, the *Droits de l'Homme* having almost three times his fire-power and at least five times his man-power. But he had that quality of all the great captains, a cool head amid tumult, which could assess the enemy's situation as accurately as his own. He had seen the topmasts fall, and knew how that would handicap the handling of the Frenchman; he knew she was overcrowded and overloaded, and he saw the rising tempest as an ally; in such a sea the lower ports of the 74 would have to be kept shut, only opened briefly when the guns were ready to fire; a serious drawback for that formidable battery of 32-pounders. Above all, he knew his men and they knew him; there was complete mutual confidence; the battle was only to be won by discipline and seamanship, and his men knew well that there was no more consummate seaman afloat than Sir Edward Pellew.

The INDEFATIGABLE came up with the *Droits de l'Homme* about 5.30 p.m., as darkness was falling; shortened sail to close-reefed topsails only, drew across the enemy's stern and opened with a raking broadside, to which there could be no immediate reply; the battleship, however, was able to draw alongside, and pour in her powerful broadside, as well as a very heavy fire of musketry from the soldiers on board. Pellew now drew ahead, intending to cross the bows of his opponent and rake her again; this attempt was foiled, and the *Droits de l'Homme* tried to run him down and board with her six hundred soldiers; but the INDEFATIGABLE evaded and continued the cannonade.

The AMAZON had been about eight miles astern when Sir Edward commenced the action, but made for the gun-flashes under all the sail she could carry; she came up at about 6.45 p.m., fired a broadside at close range into the quarter of the *Droits de l'Homme*, and tried to pass under her stern to rake her with the other broadside, but with great skill Commodore la Crosse so manœuvred as to bring both his antagonists together on his weather side, where the heeling of his ship enabled him to open his lower-deck ports. Such a broadside was more than frigates could stand, and at 7.30 p.m. both British ships went on ahead; the AMAZON because she had too much sail on, which she could not shorten during the engagement, and the INDEFATIGABLE to repair her rigging and sway up more shot from her hold. The *Droits de l'Homme* was very glad of the respite, for one of her 24-pounders on her upper deck had just burst, no doubt due to a breaking wave having stopped the muzzle with water just as the gun was fired. A gun-burst is as bad an accident as can happen; apart from the actual casualties caused by a 2½-ton gun flying into fragments, every other gunner thinks his gun may be next.

At 8.30 p.m. the British ships re-engaged, and the desperate action continued for almost the whole of the winter's night. No bald description can give the slightest idea of the scene; the howling of the gale, the tossing of the ships, the thunder and flame of the guns, the crashing of the shot and the incessant musketry. The frigates stationed themselves as well as they could, one on each bow of the battleship, where their broadside could rake her with best effect and she could not bring her great batteries to bear. By yawing first on one side and then on the other she was able to fire at least her forward guns into the frigates, and was always intent on the least chance to run in and board, which must have been decisive; but the seamanship of both the frigate captains frustrated every attempt.

The wind veered to the westward again, still rising. So high ran the sea, that in the INDEFATIGABLE the gun-crews on the main deck were waist-deep in water; and in the *Droits de l'Homme*, every time they opened the lower ports to fire the 32-pounders, the water poured down on to the prisoners in the cable tier. So violent was the tossing that several of the main deck guns of the INDEFATIGABLE broke the ropes of their breeching-tackle, and others drew the ring-bolts out of the ship's side; the force of the recoil added to the tossing of the ship being more than any sane shipwright could be expected to think about. A gun breaking loose in a tempest was the ultimate disaster; Sir Edward, who thought of everything, had thought of this too, and had ordered such a quantity of spare rope to be rove that every accident was dealt with immediately it occurred.

The fire of the frigates was deadly among the French gun-crews; but as fast as they fell others took their place, whether sailors or soldiers; no Frenchman hung back. At 10.30 p.m. the mizzen-mast of the *Droits de l'Homme* was observed to be tottering, and shortly after Commodore la Crosse ordered it to be cut away, so as to fall clear of the deck. The driver, the main fore-and-aft sail of the ship, was rigged on the mizzen, and this loss made the ship very difficult to manage. The British frigates now took station on the quarters of the battle-ship, where their fire had even greater effect, as it was on the quarter-deck that most of the officers had their station. Several of them were wounded; on the other side, Lieutenant Bendall Littlehales, first of the AMAZON, was promenading the quarter-deck with his captain when he was knocked unconscious by the wind of a 32-pound shot from the lower-deck battery of the *Droits de l'Homme*. Captain Reynolds had him carried below; as soon as he came round he insisted on returning to his post; but it was months before the bruising disappeared: one of the earliest examples of super-sonic shock.

Shortly after midnight the *Droits de l'Homme* had fired off all her round-shot and started firing shell, which, according to her log, made the British stand off a little further. She must have fired at least 4,000 rounds to have exhausted her shot, all 24 or 32 pounds. By four o'clock in the morning of the 14th January, exhaustion was beginning to show, after eleven hours of furious combat under the worst possible conditions. The AMAZON had three feet of water in her hold, only the stump of her mizzen-mast standing, all her other masts and yards seriously damaged, and she had repaired her rigging so often that she had not a yard of spare cordage left. Her casualties, however, were only three killed and fifteen wounded. The INDEFATIGABLE had four feet of water in her hold, and all her masts damaged, although, by the diligence of her crew, still standing; she had no killed and nineteen wounded. It was far different on the *Droits de l'Homme*, where there were 103 killed and 150 wounded.

Still the exhausted crews stood to their guns, and still the fury of the cannonade thundered out over the fury of the tempest; until at half-past four a break in the flying clouds allowed the moon to enlighten the scene, and Lieutenant George Bell, fourth of the INDEFATIGABLE, whose action station was on the forecastle, saw land dead ahead to the north-east, less than two miles away and with breakers in front of it. By the time he could get to the quarter-deck with this news the breakers were clearly seen from there. Pellew's appreciation of the situation was instantaneous; thinking of everything, he ordered the signal for imminent danger to be made to the AMAZON; ordered his lieutenants to cease fire, and his sailing-master to put the ship about across the wind. One can imagine the thoughts of the exhausted crew as the successive orders came through: 'Cease fire! Hands to the braces! Stand by to go about!' Everybody knew what was involved.* In such weather the amount of sail carried must be exactly right; if too much, the ship would be dismasted and drive ashore; if too little, as she turned into the wind she would lose steerage-way and broach-to in the trough of the waves. Very well:

* There is always a certain amount of tension at such times. The author had twice occasion to put his little 60-tonner about in heavy weather, in a gale, force 8, in the Irish Sea, and in a hurricane, force 12, in the Firth of Forth. The difference in pitch between the howl of the gale and the shriek of the hurricane is quite remarkable.

but what of her shot-through masts, her cut rigging, her torn sails? Would she stand? Orders were given and carried out as steadily as if at sail drill in Spithead; round she swung into the wind, hung in stays for a sickening moment, and then with a thunderous clapping the close-reefed top-sails filled on the other tack, and she sped away from the breakers like a frightened gull. Not so her consort; not so her enemy. Lacking her mizzen-mast and driver, the AMAZON could not bear up into the wind; she tried to wear round with it, but had not sea-room enough, and before five o'clock ran ashore. The *Droits de l'Homme* tried to bear up into the wind, but instantly her foremast and bowsprit carried away, leaving only the torn mainsail standing; she tried to anchor, but the anchor would not hold, and shortly she struck heavily on a sandbank; struck again, carrying away her mainmast with the shock; swung broadside on to the sandbank, struck again, turned on her side and remained fast, with the great seas breaking right over her.

The INDEFATIGABLE was far from safe. This glimpse of land had looked like the island of Ushant, and there was plenty of sea-room on her new course, if that were the case. But at first light breakers were seen ahead again, and there was nothing for it but to go about again. Dawn came about half-past six, and again breakers were seen ahead, and again she had to go about. As the light improved, the AMAZON was seen ashore, and, two miles south, the *Droits de l'Homme* on her side, with a great surf beating right over her. No attempt at rescue could be contemplated, for now they could make out where they were: right in the dangerous Bay of Audierne, and ahead of them Penmarck Point, with the dreaded Penmarck Rocks around it, the breakers leaping to top-mast height. But the situation, though desperate, could at least be seen; no more knocking about in the darkness from one hazard to another. For four, mortal hours the worn-out sailors toiled at the ropes, beating up against the relentless storm, desperately clawing off the spouting reefs; until at eleven o'clock the INDEFATIGABLE cleared the last of the rocks and stood out to the open sea.

Shortly after the AMAZON struck, six of her crew stole a small boat and tried to go off on their own; but she soon swamped and all six were drowned. Captain Reynolds set his men to

constructing rafts, and when there was flotation for everybody the whole ship's company including the wounded were enrafted and drifted to shore, where they all arrived safely by nine o'clock that morning, having struck about five. Of course they became prisoners of war.

Things were quite different on board the *Droits de l'Homme*. One of the English prisoners taken off the Shannon, Lieutenant Pipon, wrote a long account of the wreck. As soon as she struck the prisoners were brought up from the cable tier to the deck. They could see the AMAZON on shore, about two miles away, and to seaward the INDEFATIGABLE, beating off the Penmarcks under close-reefed topsails in a tremendous sea; from the *Droits de l'Homme*, she appeared to be doomed. On board the French ship all was chaos, men rushing about screaming and shouting without any apparent purpose; the same men who had served their guns so steadily during the most bloody battle seemed now to be quite unnerved. The officers had given up all command and responsibility, and the men's only thought was *sauve qui peut*. As a consequence, although the wreck was scarcely two hundred yards from the shore, where hundreds of people had assembled from the adjacent town of Plouzoneo, it was five days until the rescue was completed, and two-thirds of the survivors of the battle perished of starvation and exposure.

This was the last frigate action fought by Sir Edward Pellew. When next we hear of him, he was in command of a squadron of line-of-battle ships. About the time of Trafalgar he was for some years Rear-Admiral, Commander-in-Chief, East Indies. After the death of Lord Collingwood, Vice-Admiral Sir Edward Pellew, Bart., became Commander-in-Chief, Mediterranean, flying his flag in the new CALEDONIA of 120 guns, having

Position in Audierne Bay, 8 a.m., 14th January 1797

1 AMAZON ashore; crew prepared to enraft
2 *Droits de l'Homme* on her side, dismasted; panic on board
3 INDEFATIGABLE beating to windward under double-reefed topsails only

If more detail is required, the appropriate Admiralty Chart is No. 2351. There is a detailed description of the Bay in the Channel Pilot, Part II.

with him on board—surprise!—Rear-Admiral Israel Pellew as Captain of the Fleet. He finished the wars as Admiral Viscount Exmouth, Knight Grand Cross of the Order of the Bath, and reputed to have amassed £300,000 in prize-money. His descendants bear his title to this day. But amongst all his well-won honours and rewards, the story men always told of him was how the INDEFATIGABLE fought a French 74 in a tempest the whole of a winter's night, ran her on shore, and then weathered the Penmarcks. It was a feat of arms and seamanship such as had never been done before, and never was done again.

3

Mutiny and Retribution

A verity that enthusiasts forget is that things keep on happening, even after the most resounding victory or the most disastrous defeat, and very seldom do they happen as expected. When the British were rejoicing over Wolfe's conquest of Canada, it did not occur to anybody that it made inevitable the secession of the American Colonies; and when Louis XVI triumphantly signed the treaty which finally established the United States, he did not know that he was signing his own death-warrant for nine years later. Such an explosion as the French Revolution had a world-wide fall-out, and while Britain was at war with the Republic, nevertheless the ideas of the revolution spread and took root. British sailors would fight and run ashore the *Droits de l'Homme*; but they might reflect that they too were men and possibly they too had rights. Then the numbers in the Navy had been expanded from 20,000 to 120,000, so that five out of six were recent recruits or conscripts, and among them, we may be sure, were many on whom the ideas of the revolutionaries had made a deep impression. There was always a sufficient cadre of commissioned officers to command any probable number of ships; but even this had its dangers, for many of the senior officers were too old, too set in their ways, to realise that fresh winds were blowing. The mutiny at Spithead was really more of a strike; the sailors had legitimate grievances, and they refused to go to sea until these were redressed. They had the full sympathy of all the younger officers such as Nelson who, however, detested the mutineers at the Nore, where politics played a part. Even after those Fleet mutinies were appeased and suppressed there were sporadic outbursts of unrest in the ships throughout the world.

It was easy enough, given Treasury approval, to meet most of the grievances: the sailors had not had a rise in pay since the rates were laid down by Samuel Pepys; the method of paying was quite archaic, so that the sailors had often to sell their warrants at a huge loss for ready money or else wait interminably for their pay in cash. The food was often much worse than necessary, and the pursers cheated the men all too often. Oddly, the most difficult problem was the demand for fresh vegetables when in port; Pepys' regulations made no mention of such a thing, and gentlemen on a well-varied diet could see no reason to introduce any such novelty. But the real root of discontent was the discovery the men had made from their prisoners—there was no flogging in the Republican Navy. The Nelson generation of officers knew that they could only lead their men, but there were still too many who thought that they could drive them; they would flog their crews into what they thought was discipline but was only subjection. At Spithead, the most objectionable officers were put ashore and declined to reassume command; Admiralty was unable to find other ships for them, and they went on half-pay for the rest of their lives. Henceforth every captain knew that his log would be carefully examined when he submitted it to Admiralty at the end of his voyage, and if a lot of floggings were recorded he would require good justification, or strong influence, if he were to get another ship. But the weeding-out took a long time; too many weak men thirsted to display their authority, and too often unbridled sadism was the compensation for the complete absence of anything like a normal sex life.

The family of Pigot was most distinguished in naval records, and for generations had given to the Navy officers noted for their bravery and efficiency; unfortunately, several of them were also noted for their severity in enforcing discipline, which in one case went far beyond the limits of standing orders, or even of sanity. The disciplinary difficulties must be recognized. A captain could not impose the death penalty, and even if he could he would only be reducing a not too numerous complement; imprisonment would scarcely be considered as a punishment, but rather as a blessed cessation from toil, even if in fetters. Extra duty might hazard the ship, since every man was already working up to the fatigue limit. Cutting off grog might be effective with really unpopular men, but in general it was evaded by the culprit's messmates making up his allowance amongst them. At the same time the highest standards of discipline had to be maintained amongst a rough illiterate body of men, of whom a high proportion were society's drop-outs. Even in 1944, it is generally believed that Major-General Wingate employed corporal punishment in his memorable 'Chindit' jungle campaign. It is quite a large problem, not to be readily solved by 'gentlemen in England now abed' whose most difficult disciplinary problem has been an encounter with an inebriated Cypriot waiter.

A flogging was a serious matter which had to be entered in the ship's log; all hands were called 'to witness punishment' and the stated offence and the sentence were read out before execution, but on a long cruise it would be years before the captain had to send in his log to Admiralty, and meantime he was in a position of absolute authority seldom granted except to sovereigns. This authority was taken for granted and seldom used by the great captains such as Nelson, Pellow, Hoste and Maxwell; they punished with the greatest reluctance, and felt that there must be some inadequacy on their part if it became necessary. Most of the modern captains followed their example, but there were a number of captains whose severity was known and dreaded throughout the fleet; consequently, they had great difficulty getting a crew together, and when they did, it was usually the sweepings from the receiving ships, whose stupidity and disaffection gave great grounds for severity at the very beginning of a commission. These severe captains fell into two categories: the hard-bitten old salts of previous wars, who felt that an occasional flogging kept the whole crew on their toes; and young captains who had come to Captain's rank far too quickly, by family influence, and whose arrogance and perversities had full play in such a position of limited but absolute command.

Of the latter type was Captain Hugh Pigot, of the 32-gun 12-pounder HERMIONE, on the West Indies station in 1797 under Sir Hyde Parker, Commander-in-Chief. Captain Pigot was a brave and efficient officer, but of a most unfortunate disposition, combining discourtesy to his officers with savage brutality to his crew. On the 22nd of March 1797 the HERMIONE carried out a neat boat-action; the ship's boats, commanded by the first and second lieutenants, Samuel Reid and Archibald Douglas, went into an anchorage of Puerto Rico, spiked and dismounted the guns of a battery guarding the anchorage, and took out thirteen prizes, including three armed privateers and a richly laden brig. In April of 1797 Captain Pigot was acting Commodore of a small squadron consisting of his own and two similar frigates, a brig and a cutter, detached to act against some privateers and their prizes which had taken refuge in Port Jean-Rabel, in San Domingo, under the protection of two batteries. On the very dark night of the 20th–21st April all the boats of the squadron, after a long row, boarded the vessels and by 4 a.m. brought them all out on the land breeze, despite the fire of the batteries, with no loss whatever, the prizes being a full-rigged ship, three brigs, three schooners and two sloops. This was a useful and meritorious service, but in his official letter Captain Pigot did not give any name of the many lieutenants and junior officers engaged, thus, of course, depriving them of a good mark towards ultimate promotion. He himself was not personally engaged in either of these services, except in getting the lion's share of the prize-money; this was in fact according to the general rule that the captain should stay with his ship and send his lieutenants in the boats, but it was also the general rule that in such cases the captain should take all the trouble necessary to see that they got full credit.

On the 22nd September 1797 Captain Pigot was cruising in the HERMIONE off the west end of Puerto Rico; deciding to shorten sail, he ordered the topsails to be reefed. When the top-men were on the mizzen-topsail yard, directly over the quarter-deck, he shouted at them that he would flog the last man off the yard. It is difficult to believe that his mind was not quite unbalanced when he made this threat, for not only are the top-men the best sailors in the ship, but the best of them take the outside ends of the yards, at the clew-earrings, so that inevitably it must be the best men who are last off the yard. One thing they could be sure of, and that was that the captain would carry out his threat. As they were all rushing down the rigging, the two yard-men, finding their way blocked, made a leap through the air, hoping to catch hold of some part of the rigging lower down. Both missed, and both crashed at the same time on to the quarter-deck. The boatswain and the sailing-master examined them and reported to the captain that they were both dead. 'Throw the lubbers overboard,' was all the captain said, and it was done.

Nobody knows what was thought on board the HERMIONE that evening. The captain, alone in his cabin must have reflected, if he were not in fact insane, that he had two lives to account for and a very poor account to give. The first lieutenant and the sailing-master must have been wondering what the captain was going to write in the log, and whether they dared to share his guilt by signing it (as was their duty), or whether they dared to defy him by refusing to sign it (as was their duty also). There cannot have been much gay talk and happy laughter in either ward-room or gun-room; forward, there were 'low whispers and black frowns'. Apart from the psychotic sadism of the captain, which had already driven them as far as men could be driven, the whole crew felt the insult of their murdered comrades being hove overboard to the sharks. They expected their dead to be treated with proper ceremony; sewn up in canvas by the sail-maker's mates, with a couple of round-shot at the feet; laid out on the gratings on the gangways, and the burial service read over them; the gratings tilted till the bodies slid overside, to the wail of the pipes. To throw them overboard like galley-slops was the ultimate insult, after the ultimate injury of a causeless death. They would take no more.

As the night came on, dark and moonless, the watch on deck began rolling round-shot about the deck. This was very often the precursor of mutiny; even a 12-pound shot would 'take the feet' from anybody walking on the deck who met it, while the barefooted sailors could make their way anywhere without touching the deck. The trundling of the shot caused the first lieutenant to come out to see what was amiss; he was wounded in the arm with a hatchet, and then hacked down, his throat cut, and his body thrown overboard. On hearing the tumult, the captain ran out, but was driven back into his cabin (the Marine sentry taking no action) where he was stabbed by his own coxswain, and after several cutlass-wounds was pushed out of the cabin window, still alive. No officer attempted to interfere, but the mutineers now entered the ward-room and killed all the ward-room officers most bloodily with axes and cutlasses: not a shot was fired. Those murdered in the ward-room were the other two lieutenants, the lieutenant of Marines, the purser and the surgeon. The mutineers then went down to the gun-room, where they murdered in the same way the boatswain, a midshipman, and the captain's clerk. All the bodies were immediately thrown overboard, whether quite dead or not.

The only warrant officers allowed to survive were the sailing-master, the gunner, the cook, the carpenter, and one little midshipman. It was clear that they could not navigate the ship without the sailing-master, nor fight an action without the gunner; do repairs without the carpenter, nor subsist without the cook; but why the midshipman was spared is a mystery. Perhaps even in that night of fear and horror some gleam of pity fell on the poor boy.

It might possibly have been the original intention of at least some of the mutineers merely to detain the captain in his cabin and then desire the first lieutenant to take the ship to the Admiral at Jamaica. The possibility might then exist that they might have been forgiven, especially if the captain was held to be insane; but once the first lieutenant was wounded every man on board was under sentence of death, or what was worse, flogging round the fleet. The systematic murder of the officers does not seem the outcome of panic or blind rage, since they carefully preserved those who were indispensable to them. They killed everybody they could do without, and whose testimony might later help to convict them.

Perhaps they had some idea of making off to the great South Seas, like the BOUNTY's men, but they must soon have been convinced that they were not victualled nor equipped for either the voyage round the Horn against the weather, or for 15,000 miles on the route round the Cape of Good Hope. They may have thought of turning pirates, but in the West Indies every man's hand would have been against them; all the warships and privateers of both sides. Eventually they decided to surrender the ship to the Spaniards, now at war with Britain, and they obliged the sailing-master to take her into La Guayra, on the north coast of South America.

Here they handed the ship over to the Spanish Governor, stating that they had turned their officers loose in a boat; but the surviving warrant officers would have none of this, dissociated themselves from the crew, and insisted on being made prisoners of war. They made the truth clear to the Governor, and as news leaked out the nearest British Admiral made a formal demand for the ship and the mutineers to be handed over to him. However, the Governor fitted out the *Hermione* as a Spanish frigate with a Spanish crew, and let the mutineers go free, although it does not appear that he did anything to help them. They led an Ishmaelite kind of existence, harried wherever the power of Admiralty could extend, especially after 1808 when the Spaniards changed side again. Those who could, took service with the navy of the United States; but sooner or later, over the next twenty years, most of them were hunted down and hanged. There could be no mercy shown for such a crime, yet some pity might be felt for the perpetrators. They were the scum and scrapings of the sea-service, yet if they had fallen into the hands of Sir Sydney Smith or Lord Cochrane something might have been made of them; but such commanders could pick and choose from hundreds of volunteers. It was inevitable that the worse crews should fall to the worse commanders, and that a really bad commander should drive his crew into despair and desperation.

The Spaniards gave the *Hermione* a thorough refit and put more guns into her, making the total 44. There were comparatively few ships-of-war in the Caribbean, for its extent (twenty degrees of latitude and thirty of longitude), and a powerful frigate like this was a constant menace not only to British merchant vessels but also to the numerous small ships-of-war which were always in employment, on convoy duty and putting down privateers and pirates. It was not for two years that definite and useful information about the *Hermione* reached Sir Hyde Parker, then Commander-in-Chief at Jamaica; she had sailed from Les Cayes in San Domingo, and was now lying in Puerto Cabello, in Venezuela, about seventy miles west of Caracas. It was believed that from that port she was next to sail to Havana.

Captain Edward Hamilton was on the Jamaica station, in command of the 28-gun frigate SURPRISE. This had been a French 24-gun corvette, but on capture had been armed almost entirely with carronades, mostly 32-pounders, which made her a formidable ship at close quarters, but a sitting duck for any long-gun frigate which could keep out of range of her carronades. To help her speed, Captain Hamilton (who seems to have been on good terms with the Dockyard) had her fitted with the mainmast and yards appropriate to a 36-gun frigate. When the news about the *Hermione* was known, Captain Hamilton proposed to the C-in-C that he should be given an extra twenty men and another boat, and he would try to cut out the *Hermione* by boarding from boats; but Sir Hyde Parker, always more noted for caution than for dash, turned it down. However, when Captain Hamilton sailed next day on sealed orders, he found that they were to proceed to Cabo de la Vela, west of the Gulf of Venezuela, and about 200 miles west of Puerto Cabello; he was to cruise off the Cape as long as his stores would allow, and in particular to look out for the *Hermione*, which would be bound to follow the channel between the Lesser Antilles and the mainland, if sailing for Havana. It was highly typical of British practice to send a 28-carronade ship to seek out and destroy a ship of 44 long guns; but no doubt if they *had* met on the high seas the SURPRISE would have done the job.

No *Hermione* turned up, however, although the SURPRISE cruised about for some weeks, until Captain Hamilton began to fear that she must have slipped past at night; to satisfy himself, he made the long beat to windward right up to Puerto Cabello. There, sure enough, was the *Hermione*, in an impregnable position, moored head and stern so that her broadside covered the entrance, which was further strengthened by formidable batteries on either bank; when later Captain Hamilton was able to make some contact with the land, he was informed that the shore batteries mounted no less than 200 guns between them. Clearly he would be unwise to engage a force eight times more powerful than his own, especially as the long guns of the defences would shatter the SURPRISE to matchwood before any of her carronades could range. Moreover, the crew of the *Hermione*, including soldiers, was little short of 400 men, while the whole complement of the SURPRISE was less than 200. As Captain Hamilton had sailed close in, the enemy was well aware of his presence, and there was little chance of surprise; anyhow, the entrance was patrolled by gun-boats by day and by night.

All this was rather discouraging, especially to an officer who knew that he had already somewhat exceeded his orders; but being a Scot, and a Hamilton at that, the captain was unwilling to put his tail down and go home. For three days he cruised around, speaking to nobody, but writing a good deal in his cabin. On the 24th October 1799 he invited all his wardroom officers to dine with him, and was as gay as befitted a captain; then, when the cloth was drawn and the stewards had left, he told them what he was going to do, and asked for their support, for some of them were not bound to the orders he proposed: they drank his health and success resoundingly. The whole ship's company was summoned aft, and the captain addressed them from the quarter-deck. He informed his men that it was impossible to wait there any longer; the supply position would compel him to leave the station, and that frigate must become the prize of some more fortunate ship. (Deep groans and murmurs.) There was only one alternative, and he intended to take it. 'I shall cut out that frigate this very night!' (Loud cheers.) 'I shall lead the boats myself!' (Louder cheers.) 'Will you follow me?' (Loud and prolonged cheers.) 'Then listen carefully, here are my orders; I want every man to know what he is to do, his station and his officer.' The challenge was to be 'Britannia'; the answer 'Ireland'. Everybody was to be dressed in blue or dark clothes, not a rag of white or light colour. The men specifically detailed for boarding were to take the first spell at the oars, so as to be rested before they went into action; but if necessary all were to board, leaving only the bowman in each boat, to hang on if he could. The six boats were arranged in two divisions, each three being roped in tow, one division to go round the *Hermione* and attack the starboard side, the other the near or larboard side. The pinnace, with the captain, the gunner (Mr John Maxwell), a midshipman and sixteen men, was to board at the centre, on the gangway; the launch, with a lieutenant, a midshipman and twenty-four men, was to pass the pinnace and board at the starboard bow, cut the cable with axes provided, and set the fore-topsail; the little jolly-boat, with a midshipman, the carpenter, and eight men, was to board the quarter-deck, cut the stern cable, and set the mizzen-topsail. The gig, with the surgeon in command (Mr John M'Mullen) and sixteen men, was to board the larboard bow, one cutter with a lieutenant, a Marine officer, and sixteen men, was to board the larboard gangway, and the other cutter, with the boatswain and sixteen men, was to board the larboard quarter. The rendezvous was to be the quarter-deck.

These were excellent orders, the best that could be made for so desperate an enterprise. The only officer left on board was the sailing-master, being the only man who could take the ship out if the attempt was a failure, in which case few officers could be expected to rejoin. But in war there are no certainties, least of all in sea warfare; Nelson had his best captain go aground at Aboukir, and three ships at Copenhagen; not to be provided for in the most detailed orders. In this case the advancing boat-flotilla was discovered by two gun-boats, who opened fire, and some of the boats held back to engage the gun-boats. The pinnace, while rounding the *Hermione*'s bows, caught her rudder in a buoy-rope, and Captain Hamilton and his men had to scramble as best they could on to the forecastle. By this time the whole of the *Hermione*'s crew were fully alerted, mostly gathered on the main deck, whence they kept up a brisk fire of musketry on a dark mass consisting of their own gun-boats and some of the attacking boats, which they imagined to be two frigates bearing down to attack them. The captain and his party made a rush along the gangway, but on the quarter-deck some of them were borne back; the surgeon's party now advanced along the other gangway, catching the Spaniards in a cross-fire. For a time Captain Hamilton stood alone on the Spanish quarter-deck, where he was attacked by four men and knocked down by a musket-butt. At this moment the Marines boarded, and after a single volley rushed the main deck with the bayonet; all the boats, however delayed, boarded and carried out their tasks; the cables were cut; the fore-topsail and the mizzen-topsail filled on the breeze off the land; the gunner and two others, all wounded, took the wheel; and the HERMIONE stood out of Puerto Cabello. The batteries opened fire and scored several hits; the Spanish prisoners were restive down below, and the Marines had to fire down the hatchways; but when this resistance was quelled, Captain Hamilton ordered no shot to be fired and no light to be shown, and under the random fire of

200 guns the HERMIONE stood out to sea, and joined the SUR-PRISE before 3 a.m.

A striking feature of this desperate adventure was the casualty list; on the British side, none killed and twelve wounded, including the captain and the gunner; on the Spanish side, 119 killed and 97 wounded. How was this possible? How was it that sixteen men could clear the forecastle, charge along a gangway and clear the quarter-deck, before their supporting forces arrived, and in the teeth of nearly four hundred alerted men? How could thirty Marines drive below two hundred Spaniards, at the point of the bayonet? Partly the answer lay in the detailed and public orders; every man knew what he was expected to do, and was determined to do it. Another answer was that known to all great captains: the overall numbers do not matter, what matters is the number, force and quality at the point of contact. The British, on the attack, had every man his task; they were encountering only the Spaniards who happened to be there at the time, and no doubt wished themselves elsewhere. In a quick fierce rush in a confined space, the leading rank was all-important; let the first line of defenders look but just one glance over their shoulders, all fell into confusion and the action was lost.

The SURPRISE and HERMIONE arrived at Port Royal, Jamaica, on the 1st November 1799, to be acclaimed as they deserved; especially the gallant surgeon, John M'Mullen, who had no possible business to be commanding a boat in a desperate boarding action, but who in fact saved the battle: his was the only boat which carried out orders precisely, and his timely arrival and determined advance decided the quarter-deck affray.

Sir Hyde Parker took the HERMIONE into the Royal Navy, but under the name of RETALIATION; which was afterwards altered by Admiralty to RETRIBUTION. Captain Hamilton was knighted by the King; the House of Assembly of Jamaica presented him with a sword of 300 guineas value; and the City of London made him a Freeman. In the action, however, he had suffered many and serious wounds, from which he never quite recovered. He was sent home to recuperate in the ordinary packet-ship, which was captured by a French privateer and he was sent as prisoner of war to Paris. The First Consul took particular notice of Sir Edward Hamilton, and in consideration of his wounds allowed him to be exchanged for six midshipmen, and he arrived safely home in the summer of 1800, honoured by both friend and foe.

4

Invasion

On the 17th of February 1797 there slipped out from Brest a small squadron, under the command of Captain Jean-Baptiste Montaignes Laroque: it consisted of two powerful frigates, *Résistance* and *Vengeance*, both rated as 40 guns but mounting 48, a 22-gun corvette *Constance*, and a lugger, *Vautour*. The lugger was unarmed but was packed with men; they were embarked on one of the most extraordinary expeditions ever sent out.

The French Directory, in spite of the failure at Bantry Bay, still had designs of a landing in force in Ireland, and to further this decided on a demonstration against England. Raking the gaols, they picked out 1,200 men, mostly bandits and deserters, put them into uniform, gave them muskets and bayonets, and ammunition, not, however, to be distributed until after landing. The command was given to an American mercenary named Tate, who was given the rank of Colonel, and who seems to have been admirably suited for such a command. His orders were to land at Bristol, sack and burn the city, and then march overland to Liverpool, sacking and burning *en route*. No arrangements were made for taking the party off. They had no cannon, no camp equipment, no transport, and no supplies. The men were promised a free pardon and all the loot they could lay their hands on. Quite clearly, the Directory considered the party expendable.

On the 20th of February the squadron anchored off Ilfracombe, where some attempt at a landing was abandoned on news of organised resistance. The commodore had probably got some information about the tides and currents of the Bristol Channel, for he gave up that objective and sailed north, anchoring in Fishguard Bay towards dusk on 22nd February. The stop at Ilfracombe was of course imbecilic; nothing was accomplished, and on the other hand the alarm was given, and all round the coast the militia were assembling. During the night all the 1,200 men were landed, and having got rid of them, the squadron made off immediately.

During that night the local magnate, Lord Cawdor, assembled the local Yeomanry, Militia, and Volunteers, and by full day marched to meet the invaders. Seeing the ordered lines of resolute men, and especially, no doubt, the cavalry, of which he had none, 'Colonel' Tate at once put up the white flag and surrendered. Not a drop of blood was shed. It has been said that Tate was further influenced by mistaking some red-shawled women for soldiers, and a correspondent of the *Daily Telegraph* (19th February 1969) has said that this was in fact a ruse organised by Lord Cawdor, who issued the women with a yard and a half of military scarlet apiece and set them to march round and round a hillock, like a stage army.

This expedition, however ludicrous it seems at this distance, did in fact have one of the effects the Directory hoped for: it caused a run on the banks, which had already been under increasing pressure. This became so serious that on the 26th of February an Order in Council was issued, authorising the Bank of England to issue £1 and £2 notes as legal tender, and this Order was subsequently legalised by Act of Parliament. This important step, which would never have been taken under ordinary conditions, was of the greatest benefit to the war effort; paper money freely accepted freed the country's gold for the foreign subsidies without which the war must have collapsed.

The second effect was that the British public, seeing the miserable condition and behaviour of these 'troops', at once concluded that all French soldiers were miserable, cowardly, half-starved tramps, an illusion which was rudely dispelled by the splendid armies of Napoleon.

At dawn on the 9th of March 1797 two British frigates made a reconnaissance of Brest Roads. They were the SAN FIORENZO, 36 guns, 18-pounders, Captain Sir Harry Neale, and the NYMPHE, 36 guns, 12-pounders, Captain John Cooke. Having ascertained that the French fleet, fourteen battleships and six frigates, was still in the port, they were returning to inform

Lord Bridport, commanding the Channel Fleet off Ushant, when they sighted two sails to the westward, apparently making for Brest. The complication was that Brest was only ten miles away, and the wind was fair for leaving the port, so that anything to be done must be done quickly before overwhelming force could be brought out.

The two British frigates hauled close to the wind until they had the weather-gauge of the enemy, and then bore down on the leading ship, which was the *Résistance*, with the commodore of the Fishguard expedition; she did not resist long, however, but after an engagement of about ten minutes hauled down her colours and was taken into possession. The second ship now arrived, the corvette *Constance*, Captain Desauney, and was in a hopeless position, but made a spirited fight for ten minutes, until she lost her mainmast and surrendered. The frigate had nineteen casualties, the corvette fourteen; the British ships had no damage and no casualties.

The *Résistance* was one of the finest frigates afloat, nearly 1,200 tons, and was taken into the Royal Navy under the appropriate name of FISGARD; rated as a 38-gun frigate, she did excellent service for a long period. The *Constance* was also taken into service, under her own name, and was rated as a 22-gun post-ship. Thus the net result of the Fishguard expedition was to save the Bank of England, to present the Royal Navy with two fine ships, and to confer a nice bit of easy prize-money on two lucky ships' companies.

It is perhaps to be remarked that this was the very last time that an armed enemy force ever stood on the soil of the Island.

5

The East India Station:
The Far East

Edward Cooke was fortunate in his education. As a very young
lieutenant, he had spent quite a part of the ten years' peace
between 1783 and 1793 in France, with the special intention
of learning the language. (Nelson had intended to do the
same, but was deterred by the senile entreaties of his father
for his company.) By the time he was recommissioned in 1793,
he was not only proficient but perfect in the language of the
enemy. He quickly attracted the keen eye of Vice-Admiral
Lord Hood, who had him as one of his lieutenants on his flag-
ship, the VICTORY, when he sailed for Toulon in the middle of
1793, with another twenty ships of the line and a sufficiency
of frigates and small craft. To be a lieutenant on a flag-ship,
with its strict ceremonial and constant calls, was perhaps not
much fun, but it was regarded as an almost certain promise
of early promotion, so long as one did not attract the unfa-
vourable attention of the Admiral.

The situation at Toulon was quite tricky: the citizens and
the Councillors were almost all Monarchists, and so was the
Rear-Admiral Trogoff, commanding the fleet in the harbour;
but the sailors deposed him and elected Rear-Admiral Julien,
a strong Revolutionary. Lord Hood was given to understand
that the city authorities were willing to treat for the condi-
tional surrender of the town and the fleet, and he sent his best
French-speaking officer, Lieutenant Cooke, ashore to conduct
these extremely delicate negotiations. It was quite remarkable
that out of a fleet carrying six flag officers and about forty post
captains, a lieutenant should be sent on such a mission, not

as interpreter but as plenipotentiary. It was sufficiently hazardous, for the Revolutionary fleet lay in the way; Cooke had to make two calls, with a day between, and on each of the four passages he had his difficulties. For instance, on his second return a French frigate saw him (rowing himself) and lowered a boat to intercept him; and, when this failed, fired upon him several times with her whole broadside, as he scampered along the beach from rock to rock and up the steep way to the cover of some trees. He was probably the only man ever to have half a dozen broadsides of a frigate directed against his single person.

With such a background, it is not surprising that five years later Edward Cooke found himself not only a post captain, but in command of one of the finest frigates in the Navy, and on the East Indies station, where there was plenty of action and plenty of prizes. His ship was the SYBILLE, rated as 38 guns but actually mounting 46; she was French-built in Toulon, of what was then called Adriatic oak, now called Jugo-Slavian, still the finest oak in the world. Every captain thirsted to command a Toulon-built capture. SYBILLE had been captured in the Mediterranean by the ROMNEY, 50 guns, on 17th June 1794.

The main base of the East Indies was at Fort St George, Madras, where a powerful force was established, sufficient to send out several detachments at a time as requisite, but always keeping a strong reserve in case of some unexpected move by the enemy. The purpose was to protect the immense convoys of the Honourable East India Company's ships from China, Indonesia and India, and of course to do as much depredation as possible on French and Dutch warships and convoys. Ships were also stationed at Calcutta, to cover the Bay of Bengal, and at Bombay, to look after shipping in the Arabian sea, where Arab pirates were the chief danger. Britain's only ally in these waters was Portugal, which had a port at Goa, not much use when Bombay was so near, and at Macao, of the very greatest service, since the great China convoys assembled at Canton, a little way upriver. Portugal also had part of the island of Timor, but this was a little out of the trade routes.

The French had had land settlements at many places on the coast of India, but these were all seized by the British shortly after news of the declaration of war was received; only Pondicherry, which was heavily fortified, made a respectable resistance. The main French naval base was at Port Louis, on the Île de France, now Mauritius, about a thousand miles SW by W from Madras. This was deemed impregnable, owing to the reefs which surrounded the island on all sides except off the heavily fortified entrance to Port Louis. Here a large naval force was stationed, mostly of powerful frigates, to protect French commerce, that of the Dutch, and of course to prey on the traffic of the Honourable East India Company. Holland had already lost to the British the Cape of Good Hope and Ceylon, and her bases were principally on Java, Batavia (now Djakarta) at the west end, and Gresik (now Sourabaya) at the east end; they had several line-of-battle ships, 64s, and a number of frigates, but showed little inclination to risk them outside Indonesian waters. Spain had an important naval base at Manila, but she was principally concerned with the Pacific, and any of her goods passing through the Indian Ocean were carried by the French Philippines Company.

The area of the East India command thus extended about six thousand by five thousand miles, including the most valuable trading countries in the world, and containing several enemy naval forces, some of them very active and aggressive: 'ample room, and verge enough' for the most ambitious officer.

Late in 1797 Cooke was sent to China, to convoy to Fort St George the fleet of the Honourable Company, then assembling at Canton. He was given also the small 32-gun 12-pounder frigate FOX, Captain Pulteney Malcolm, a man after his own heart, who also was a competent French linguist; and a pilot for the dangerous China seas, Mr Bernard, who spoke both French and Spanish; he shipped in the FOX, which, with her shallower draught, was intended to be the leading ship in tricky waters. They duly arrived at Macao at New Year, but found that the India fleet, although almost ready, did not intend to sail until March, as the monsoon period was upon them, when constant stormy weather was to be expected, varied with typhoons of the utmost violence. This did not daunt the frigate captains, who had never experienced a typhoon, and they determined to perform some service rather than lie idle at Macao, which they knew would be bad for the morale as well as the morals of their crews. They took on board a good supply of fresh beef and vegetables, and on the 5th of January sailed with the intention of reconnoitring Manila; they felt that their C-in-C would be pleased to have a reliable report, and the possibility exists that they may have been influenced by the alleged presence there of two ships of rich lading, bound for Panama.

They duly sighted the island of Luzon some distance north of their destination, and coasted southwards. They were flying French colours, and captured a small vessel which had just left Manila. The master of this ship informed his captors that in Manila there were four ships of the line and four frigates, but only one battleship and one frigate were fit for sea, the others being under repair during the monsoon season. In consideration of this information, Captain Cooke let the ship and lading go free, only robbing the till of about 4,000 Spanish dollars. The two captains now laid their plans for entering Manila Bay; they decided to be a detachment from Rear-Admiral Sercey's squadron, the SYBILLE to be the *Seine*, and the FOX the *Prudente*. On the 13th January 1798 they arrived at Manila Bay towards evening.

Manila has a large bay, about twenty miles each way, formed by the projecting peninsula of Bataan on the westward side. The city of Manila lies at the head of the bay, fairly open, although protected by a mole; but about ten miles to the south the curving peninsula of San Roque forms the magnificent harbour of Cavite, two miles deep, which was the naval base, dockyard and arsenal. Both the city and the dockyard were heavily fortified and quite recently strengthened, for in the war of 1762 the British had captured Manila by a surprise attack from India. The Manila galleon was the longed-for mark of every warship, privateer or pirate in those waters, but it was only taken once, by Commodore Anson in June 1743, who brought the CENTURION into Spithead with two millions sterling in gold and silver. It is not generally understood that fifty years before Drake entered the South Seas, the Spaniards were running a regular liner service across the Pacific: one ship a year in each direction. From Acapulco they ran along the 13° north line of latitude (very convenient before longitude could be calculated) for 8,000 miles till they came to Guam, rising out of the great deeps (5,000 fathoms) to over 1,300 feet, a fine landfall; here they refreshed before sailing the remaining 1,500 miles to Manila, the whole voyage on the North Equa-

Batan Peninsula

MANILA
BAY

Corregidor
Island

Caballe
Island

0 5 10 15 20
SEA. MILES

Pasig River

Mole

MANILA
CITY

3

2

1

Sangley Point

San Roque Peninsula

CAVITE

4

5

6

0   1   2   3
SEA MILES

torial trade wind. Returning, they stood away north into at least 30° north, where they picked up the North Pacific trade wind which carried them securely to the coast of Mexico. Manila was the entrepôt where all the riches of the East were assembled to lade the galleon.

The entrance to the bay is about ten miles wide, and contains the fortified island of Corregidor and the smaller one of Caballo. The frigates passed through unchallenged in the darkness, and before midnight anchored in the bay. At first light on the 14th January they weighed anchor and started up the bay, on a very light wind. By 9 a.m. the FOX was sufficiently advanced to see into Cavite harbour, at a distance of three miles, and descry three sail of the line and three frigates; none of them, however, ready for sea, since two of them had all their topmasts struck and the other four had all their masts out. The wind now died away altogether, leaving the frigates becalmed about half-way between Manila and Cavite, and about five miles from the shore of the bay between those places.

At 11 a.m. a twelve-oar guard-boat was observed approaching; it came alongside, and a Spanish captain came on board to make the usual inquiries. Mr Bernard told him that he was on board the *Prudente,* and the larger consort was the *Seine;* they had been detached from the squadron of Rear-Admiral Sercey to cruise on the China coast, and had come in for fresh provisions, and to find if any part of the Spanish squadron would like to join them. The Spanish captain told them that the Governor had already directed that all their requirements should be supplied, but he did not think any of the warships in the port would be able to go to sea for at least two months; which was very good hearing for the British officers.

The head of Manila Bay, 10 a.m., 14th January 1798

Reference:
1 SYBILLE, hove-to
2 FOX, hove-to
3 Three Spanish gun-boats, manned, anchored off Pasig River
4 Three Spanish line-of-battle ships, under repair
5 Three Spanish frigates, under repair
6 Two Spanish merchant ships, one unloading, one aground

Note: ships are *not* on the same scale as the map.

Inset: General view of Manila Bay, on smaller scale

Captain Cooke now came on board and was introduced as Commodore Latour, a well-known officer in Sercey's squadron; Latour had actually been dead for some time, but as the news had not yet reached Manila, everything went down very well. Captain Malcolm now invited the officers to have some wine in his cabin, and suggested that the boat's crew should come on board and have some refreshment forward. This was accepted, and while the officers had an instructive chat in the cabin, the men were shown down to the lower deck, where as they came off the ladder one at a time they were seized, disarmed and tucked away in the orlop. After about an hour, in which they pumped the Spaniard dry of all available information and replaced it with Madeira, the two British captains disclosed their identity, to the astonishment and horror of the Spanish captain. However, Captain Cooke assured him that he would not be taken away as a prisoner, and urged him to have another glass.

Meantime two large twenty-oar boats approached, bringing the Governor's nephew, and one of the aides of Admiral Alaba, commanding at Cavite, with all hospitable intentions. The officers were shown into the cabin and informed that they were temporary prisoners, while the crews were shown below and dealt with as before. But now a large party of British sailors required the Spaniards to exchange clothes with them; they then entered the three row-boats and made for three large gun-boats, which lay off the mouth of the river Pasig, which then bounded the city. Taken completely by surprise, the gun-boat crews surrendered without firing a shot, and were duly brought alongside the FOX. The gun-boats were in excellent condition, each with thirty oars and a heavy gun in the bows, one 32- and two 24-pounders, with four swivels apiece.

A fourth boat now came alongside, and the Captain of the Port came aboard, to inquire what was going on, and to demand the instant restoration of the gun-boats; otherwise the frigates would be treated as enemies. Talking volubly but not very understandably, Captain Malcolm escorted him to the cabin, while his crew were invited below. It was now 4 p.m., the dinner hour of the period, and Captain Malcolm regaled his captive officers with the best his stores could provide, and at the same time ordered a good meal and copious grog for his two hundred prisoners forward. Festivities over, all the prisoners were escorted to their boats, and allowed to go ashore without parole or conditions of any kind; but the British captains thought it a good idea to retain the gun-boats as a souvenir of their visit.

A good wind came up, and the two frigates left the bay, with the three gun-boats in tow, with prize crews. They were not unhappy; they had exposed the inherent weakness of Spanish rule in the Pacific, although it was to be exactly a hundred years until Commodore Dewey destroyed the Spanish fleet at Cavite and the U.S.A. annexed the Philippines. They had acquired a great deal of valuable information; they had not taken their merchantmen, which were well into the safety of Cavite, either aground or unladen, but they had three large copper-bottomed gunboats, three heavy brass guns, a dozen swivels, and an amplitude of small arms and ammunition; and not a drop of blood had been shed on either side. An interesting day; and all because both captains could speak French!

Note: The subsequent short career of Captain Cooke will be found in Chapter 6, 'Bay of Bengal'. Captain Pulteney Malcolm had a long and honourable career in the Royal Navy. In 1809 he commanded the DONE-GAL, 74, under Admiral Gambier off the Basque Roads; and in 1829 Admiral Pulteney Malcolm was Commander-in-Chief, Mediterranean.

6

East Indies: Bay of Bengal

Really large frigates, mounting 24-pounder guns in the main battery, were very scarce in 1799. The first was the *Pomone*, captured in 1794 (page 16) which gave Admiralty quite a shock; they cut down three 64-gun ships by one deck, and laid down the ENDYMION on the same lines as the *Pomone*. The U.S.A. had three, which had been laid down as 74s, quite the largest; the French had the *Romaine*, launched at Cherbourg in 1795, on the lines of the *Pomone*, and the much larger *La Forte*, launched at Rochefort in the same year. This was the largest frigate in the world, which had been built as a frigate from the keelson up. All the British 44s were in the Channel fleet, but the *Forte* was sent to Mauritius (then Île de France) where she was for a time the flag-ship of Rear-Admiral Sercey. In 1799 her main armament was thirty 24-pounder long guns, fourteen long 8-pounders, and eight bronze 32-pounder carronades, a total of 52 guns, plus eight swivels mounted on her waist bulwarks. In addition, her sides above water were thickly lined with cork covered with stout netting, the idea being to reduce the effect of splinters. Her displacement of 1,400 tons enabled her to carry her armament and protection with ease.

This formidable vessel, under the command of Captain Beaulieu-de-Long, was sent from Île de France at the end of 1798 to cruise in the Bay of Bengal and make prize of as many of the Honourable Company's ships as she might come across; there was nothing to be feared from their resistance. There was no British frigate on the station which, in the French view, could fight the *Forte*; and she could walk away from any 74. The complaints of the Honourable Company became such that something had to be done about the *Forte*, and as the sybille had completed her convoy duties and was in Madras, it was determined to send her forth to 'seek for, sink, burn or destroy' the French frigate.

sybille was still commanded by Captain Edward Cooke, whom we have seen playing pranks at Manila; this, however, was a serious matter, with every prospect of a desperate and possibly losing battle, so that he had to take stock of his capacity. The sybille was a Toulon-built capture, of 1,091 tons, rated as a 38-gun frigate, actually mounting twenty-eight 18-pounders as her main battery, with six long 9-pounders and fourteen 32-pounder carronades on her quarter-deck and forecastle; she was thus much more lightly armed than the *Forte*, and so far as the main battery was concerned, which is what really matters, she had a broadside of 268 pounds against 360 pounds in the *Forte*. In man-power she was also woefully deficient; the *Forte* was reputed to carry at least 500 men, although it was understood that this number must have been depleted by the number of prize crews she had had to furnish, to take her prizes to the Île de France. The established complement of the sybille was 297 men and boys, but this was now reduced to 221 officers and seamen, 10 boys, and 9 Marines, having no Marine officer. Her numbers were made up in various ways. Her previous consort, the fox, was cruising, and had sent a prize into Madras with a prize crew under Lieutenant Tuckey, who were very gladly received into the sybille. Captain Davies (of the Army), an aide-de-camp of the Governor-General, came as a volunteer; and the Governor-General drafted on board a detachment of the Army, from the Scots Brigade; a total of 131 supernumeraries altogether, making the total complement 371, or 74 above her establishment; a very different matter, however, from the same number of trained seamen.

The sybille sailed from Madras, northward-bound, on 19th February 1799, and on the 23rd met a cartel* going to Madras with some British prisoners out of the *Forte*'s prizes; Captain Cooke desired the cartel to accompany him into Balasore Roads, south of Calcutta, where they anchored on

---

* A cartel is a ship, usually a small prize, unarmed and flying a white flag, proceeding to an enemy port with prisoners for exchange.

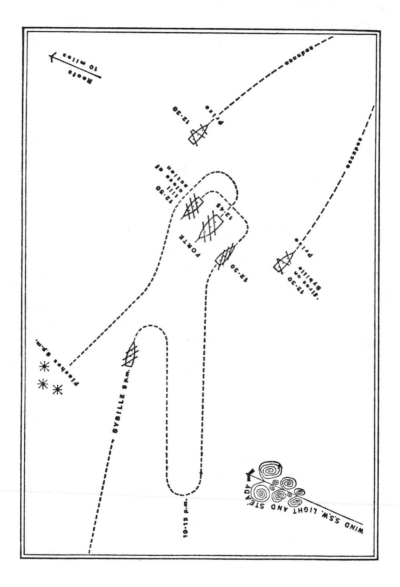

the 26th. He was unable, however, to get any positive information about the movements of the *Forte*; although he was sufficiently informed, both by the French crew of the cartel and some of the prisoners, that his ship was by no means a match for his wished-for opponent. Nothing daunted, Cooke let the cartel go on her way, while he sailed to cruise about the Sandheads off the mouth of the Hoogly river which leads up to Calcutta: this seemed a likely area in which to find a French commerce raider.

On the night of the 28th at about 8.30 p.m. the *Forte* fell in with two country ships, the ENDEAVOUR and the LORD MORNINGTON, bound from Canton for Calcutta with rich cargoes. After a desultory cannonade of about half an hour, the two surrendered and all three hove-to in the light breeze, while the *Forte* lowered boats to put prize crews on board the merchantmen and bring their officers on board the frigate. This business of 'taking possession' might require three hours or more, as the merchantmen's manifests and other documents had to be examined.

On this night, at 8.30 p.m., the SYBILLE was standing to the south-east, with a light breeze from the south-south-west, the night being very dark, when flashes were observed on the north-east horizon. This was taken to be low lightning, a common phenomenon in that area, but the steady repetition of the flashes until almost 9 p.m. aroused suspicion, and SYBILLE extinguished all lights and made sail to the westward. At 9.30 p.m. they descried three ships to the south-east, the central and largest of which they supposed to be the *Forte*; she made a most formidable appearance, her lights shining through every port; 170 feet long, she was longer than most British 74s, and with two ports in her gangways she looked exactly like a two-decker 74 which had perhaps two ports obscured. All three ships were lying-to, about two miles to the windward of the darkened SYBILLE, which stood on steadily to the westward,

Narrative: 9 p.m., SYBILLE sights flashes, and goes to windward; 10.15 p.m., enough to windward, goes about; 12.15, *Forte* leaves her prizes and turns to engage SYBILLE, opening fire at 12.30, supported by one of the prizes. SYBILLE does not reply, but turns sharply under the stern of the *Forte*, firing a broadside into it at 12.45; continues to go about, and at 12.50 fires a broadside into the starboard side of the *Forte*. The action continues in the same position until 2.30 a.m.

in order to get the weather-gauge. At 10 p.m, having got sufficiently to windward, the SYBILLE went about, furled some of her sails, and made towards the *Forte* at only two knots, under spanker, topsails and one jib only, the wind still light and steady from the SSW.

In spite of the darkness, the SYBILLE's sails must have been clearly visible on board the *Forte*; but no movement was made. What was in the captain's mind will never be known, for he had not an hour to live: one theory is that he thought the advancing ship was an East Indiaman, and lay in wait for yet another easy prize; on the other hand, British prisoners on board said that the SYBILLE was clearly recognised, but was allowed to come on as close as possible lest she should make her escape. Whatever the reason, the *Forte* made no move until just after midnight, when she squared off to the wind and advanced to the lee of the SYBILLE, firing a ragged broadside at about three-quarters of a mile range, which cut down her jib but did no other damage. One of the prizes also fired, and the *Forte* gave another partial broadside; but the SYBILLE kept steadily on, completely darkened, completely silent. One may imagine the tension on board among the officers on the quarter-deck, the sailors at the braces, the soldiers crouched behind the bulwarks, the gun-crews beside their guns: all tense, all waiting the word of command. It is at such a moment that a commander experiences the reward of all the weary months of training in which he forged the tremendous weapon to his hand.

When the stern of the *Forte* was on a line with the mainmast of the SYBILLE, Captain Cooke gave the order; the helm was put hard over, so that she passed close under the stern of her enemy, within twenty-five yards; and the whole of her larboard broadside crashed into that stern, raking the *Forte* right to the bows; still keeping the helm hard over, the SYBILLE ranged close along the lee side of the *Forte*, and crashed in a second broadside. At the same time the men of the Scots Brigade sprang to their feet, and fired across the decks of the *Forte* such a volley of musketry as she could never have expected from a British frigate.

These two broadsides from twenty-four heavy guns, plus the simultaneous volley from more than a hundred muskets, practically decided the engagement. Captain Beaulieu-de-

Long and his first lieutenant were both killed, several guns dismounted, and many of the crew killed and wounded; nevertheless the *Forte* kept up a furious and long-continued cannonade. As usual, the French fired high, perhaps higher than usually, certainly much too high, as most of their shot took effect only on the upper rigging of the SYBILLE, whose every shot crashed into the hull of the *Forte*. Nevertheless the French stuck bravely to their guns, while the flame of the cannonade illuminated the scene beneath the canopy of smoke.

At 1.30 a.m. on the 1st of March—Woe worth the day!—Captain Cooke fell, mortally wounded by a grape-shot, and the command devolved on Lieutenant Lucius Hardyman. At 1.45 a.m. Captain (Army) Davies, who had volunteered, met a 24-pound ball which nearly cut him in halves. The cannonade continued unabated for another half an hour, when the fire of the *Forte* began to slacken and ceased altogether about 2.30 a.m. The SYBILLE now stopped firing, and hailed to ask if the *Forte* had surrendered. No reply was received; SYBILLE fired another broadside, and hailed again. Again no reply was received, but now men were seen in the *Forte*'s rigging, as if setting sail with a view to escape. SYBILLE now fired continuous broadsides, and in a few minutes the mizzen-mast of the *Forte* came down, followed shortly by her foremast, mainmast and bowsprit, so that she lay a dismasted hulk. At 3 a.m. all firing ceased, and the cheers of the SYBILLE's crew were the signal for the British prisoners in the *Forte* to come on deck. Lieutenant Manger, third of the SYBILLE, was sent over by boat to take possession.

It was only after going on board that the British sailors became aware how terribly destructive had been their fire. The whole of the engaged side, above the water-line, was practically stove in; all of the bulwarks on that side had disappeared; the boats and spare spars were shot to pieces; and of all the furnishings of the deck, such as capstan, wheel and binnacle, no trace was left. Later, it was found that more than 300 shot had pierced the hull. The deck was strewn with dead and dying, a frightful spectacle; her casualties were 145 killed and wounded, including almost all the officers on board. By contrast, the SYBILLE came off lightly; she had lost most of her cordage and sails, and there were bad scars on her masts and yards, all of which were still standing; she had only six shot in her hull, and her casualties amounted to twenty-two killed and wounded.

After unsuccessfully pursuing the prizes, which made off when the outcome of the battle was plain, the SYBILLE anchored in seventeen fathoms and spent two days making such emergency repairs as enabled the two ships to make their way up the treacherous Hoogly River to Calcutta. The FORTE took a lot of repairing, but she was taken into the Royal Navy and rated as a 44-gun frigate, the largest class. Lieutenant Hardyman was given command, and this appointment was ratified by Admiralty, and Captain Hardyman made post captain. The unfortunate Captain Cooke lingered for almost three months, and died on 25th May, being of course buried with all possible military honours.

This encounter had several unique features. There was nothing unusual in the French ship having a considerable advantage in tonnage and gun-power; what is surprising is the little use she made of that superiority. Usually the French ships had much larger crews than the British, and made more use of musketry; but in this case the French had depleted the crew seriously, from 513 to 370, by the numbers she had to detach to man her prizes, which of course meant officers too; so that she had actually a man less than the British ship, and made very little use of small arms. The presence of a comparatively large body of good troops on the British ship was probably the reason, as their volley fire made the French keep their heads down. Captain Cooke was a very good officer, who had not only the confidence but the affection of officers and crew alike; moreover he had exercised his men at the guns far more than was customary at that period. The engagement is a striking illustration of the old adage, that the best defence is a rapid and accurate fire on the enemy.

7

Inglorious Defeat

The difficulties of manning the Royal Navy have already been described: by 1795 the barrel had been scraped clean of real seamen, and the Quota Acts of that year prescribed that the Justices of the Peace of each region must produce a quota of men—any kind of men—amounting to about one half per cent of the population each year. Naturally, the quota men were mostly society's discards, although there were many tempted by the handsome bounties offered to volunteers—but many of these volunteers were from debtor's prisons. By 1798, a freshly commissioned ship could be sure that most of the crew supplied from the receiving ships would be landmen of poor quality, and knocking them into the shape of seamen a difficult task for the first lieutenant and the bosun.

Such was the manning of the frigate AMBUSCADE when Captain Henry Jenkins assumed command; but she was even worse than usual, having far too large a proportion of boys. To enable the ship to be worked at all, Captain Jenkins was allowed to take a party of about thirty experienced seamen from the CARNATIC, 74, in which he had been first lieutenant; as these were volunteers, he must have been quite a popular officer, perhaps easy-going, perhaps even lax. He was certainly totally unfitted to weld a raw crew into an efficient fighting force; instead of encouraging the inexperienced to profit by the experienced, while maintaining a steady impartial discipline, he made no secret of his contempt for the original crews, whom he called 'blackguard Ambuscades', and of his partiality for the men he had brought aboard, whom he denominated 'gentlemen Carnatics'. Thus he added jealousy and distrust to the other shortcomings of his raw hands.

The AMBUSCADE was a smallish frigate of about 700 tons, 32 guns, 12-pounders, and 8 carronades, 24-pounders. She left Portsmouth on the 5th of December, 1798, to cruise on the west coast of France. She made some prizes, which had to be supplied with prize-crews, which took off her second lieutenant and twenty good sailors, leaving her with no more than 190 men and boys. On the 14th December she was lying-to off Bordeaux, waiting to be joined by the frigate STAG, 32 guns, Captain Yorke. At 7 a.m., a sail was sighted to seaward, bearing directly for them; it was taken for granted that this was the STAG, and at eight, officers and men went for breakfast, leaving only the usual watch on deck. Before 9 a.m., the approaching ship was within half a mile, when suddenly she put about and made off to sea, hauled as close to the wind as possible. This was reported to Captain Jenkins, who ordered a chase under all sail.

The ship they were chasing was the *Baionnaise*, commander Lieutenant Richer; the French called her a large corvette, the British a 28-gun frigate; she mounted twenty-four 8-pounders, six 6-pounders, and two 36-pounder carronades, plus eight swivels mounted on her bulwarks: she had thus little more than half the weight of broadside of the AMBUSCADE. She was, however, much better manned, her establishment being 280 men and boys, not all of which may have been present, as she had been to the West Indies; she had also on board a platoon of the famous regiment of Alsace, thirty men and an officer, whom she was bringing back from a tour of duty in Cayenne.

The AMBUSCADE sailed somewhat better than the *Baionnaise*, and about noon came within gunshot of her, whereupon she shortened sail and the cannonade commenced, the AMBUSCADE making full use of her heavier and longer-ranging main battery. After about an hour it appeared that the *Baionnaise* must surrender in a few minutes; she was very much knocked about in her hull, masts and rigging, and had sustained heavy casualties including both her captain and first lieutenant wounded, so that there was only one commissioned officer left to command her. The AMBUSCADE, on the other hand, had little damage and very light casualties, all her officers being still on the quarter-deck. At this moment AMBUSCADE suffered a catastrophe: one of her main deck guns burst, shattering the adjacent hull and badly wounding eleven men; such an accident is disturbing for even the best-disciplined crew, and the ill-trained men of the AMBUSCADE went into temporary panic. Taking advantage of the lull in the firing, the *Baionnaise* made sail, in the hope of escape.

The officers of the AMBUSCADE were able to quell the panic, and sail was made in pursuit; but having hoisted far more sail than was necessary to overtake a crippled opponent, she shot past and had to be brought around again to renew the engagement. During this pause the commander of the troops on board the *Baionnaise* approached the only sea officer left on the quarter-deck, with a suggestion: they had no chance in a gun duel, and could not escape by sailing; why not try boarding, and see what the regiment of Alsace was made of? 'Short time there was, ye well may guess, for musing or debate.' The suggestion was instantly adopted, and the *Baionnaise* laid on a collision course with the advancing AMBUSCADE, while the platoon fell in on the forecastle.

The attempt to board was a common manœuvre by the French, whose ships were generally much more numerously manned than the British; but it was seldom successful, as all British officers knew how to take avoiding action. Nothing would have been easier in this case than for the British, with rigging intact, to avoid the attempt and resume the cannonade; but no order was given. The captain did nothing, and nobody else dared to give an order. With a rending crash the *Baionnaise* ran into the starboard quarter of the AMBUSCADE, carrying away with her bowsprit the mizzen-mast with its rigging, the wheel, and, worst of all, the starboard bulwark of the quarter-deck, leaving it perfectly open to the fire of thirty veteran musketeers at a range of a few yards.

The British Marines on the quarter-deck stood firm, and returned the fire; with some effect, for the officer commanding the troops, who had advised the action, fell dead; but the fire of his men swept the quarter-deck. The first lieutenant, Dawson Main, received a mortal wound in the groin. Next, Captain Jenkins had part of his hip and thigh shot away, and was carried below. Lieutenant Sinclair, commanding the Marines, was wounded in thigh and shoulder. Mr Brown, the sailing-master, was shot dead through the head. In default of the second lieutenant (away with prizes), the command now devolved on the third, Joseph Briggs, who was very ill below; but he struggled up to the quarter-deck, only to be shot in his turn. Now Mr William Murray, the purser, was left in command, and of course fighting was not part of his duties; but he did his best.

At this moment a loud explosion was heard below, and an alarm of fire was raised. The gunner had ordered a gun to be shifted, in order to fire through a cabin window at the bow of the *Baionnaise*. The cartridges had been carelessly laid in such a position that the flash from the touch-hole, or perhaps an end of slow-match, ignited them, and thirty or forty pounds of gunpowder went up in a flash, blowing out part of the stern and severely burning every one of the gun's crew. Such accidents, of course, do not happen in well-run ships. This completed the panic of the crew; they bolted below, in spite of every effort of Mr Murray to rally them, and hid themselves in the bowels of the ship. The French soldiers now came over the bowsprit to the quarter-deck; the crew swarmed after them, and in a few minutes had complete possession of the AMBUSCADE.

The casualties in the AMBUSCADE were ten killed and thirty-six wounded, mostly by the two accidents related, and the fight on the quarter-deck. The *Baionnaise* had thirty killed and thirty seriously wounded plus probably as many slightly wounded, showing the effect of the fire of the AMBUSCADE, and the almost certain victory had the normal precautions to avoid being boarded been taken; four more broadsides would probably have brought the French flag down, especially since both her senior officers were below, wounded.

There was great rejoicing when the *Baionnaise* brought her prize into Rochefort, and the news was immediately spread over Europe, that a French corvette had taken a British frigate. Lieutenant Richer was given a double promotion to 'Captaine de vaisseau', which he probably merited, although he was below, wounded, when the fateful decision was taken, and took no part in the action which followed. It was, however, the greatest triumph the French Navy was to have during the twenty-two years of warfare.

The ship's company of the AMBUSCADE, now *Embuscade*, were soon exchanged, and in August of the same year a court martial sat three days at Portsmouth on the loss of the ship. Eventually the whole company was acquitted, in somewhat restrained terms. Clearly there had been rank cowardice among some of the crew, but it was very difficult to sort out the punishable from the pardonable. There had been a woeful lack of discipline and seamanship, and had Captain Jenkins been unwounded he would probably have been cashiered; but he was a poor wreck, crippled for life, who could obviously never again serve afloat. Then there was the fact that every officer of the ship had been killed or badly wounded at his post; the ship had been overwhelmed, not surrendered; she never struck her flag.

There was, of course, a sequel. On 28th May 1803 the *Embuscade* was on the last few days of a passage from the West Indies to Rochefort, just entering the Bay of Biscay. The positions of the British blockading fleets were known, and also the usual whereabouts of the patrolling frigates, so that *Embuscade* had little to fear, although she had a much depleted crew and some guns dismounted. But she was never a lucky ship. She now met with the VICTORY, 100 guns, Captain Sutton, on her way to the Mediterranean to become Nelson's flag-ship. *Embuscade* tried her heels, but VICTORY was the fastest three-decker of her day, in spite of her age (sixty-three years); to fight was out of the question, for one broadside from the VICTORY would have reduced the *Embuscade* to firewood. (The first broadside the VICTORY fired at Trafalgar, on the *Bucentaure*, 80 guns, flag-ship of Vice-Admiral Villeneuve, caused four hundred casualties, dismounted twenty guns, and left the ship practically defenceless.) There was nothing for it but to surrender, without a shot fired, and a prize crew took her to Portsmouth, where the AMBUSCADE was re-entered in the list of the Royal Navy.

On the 27th November of the same year the *Baionnaise* was cruising off the north-west coast of Spain when she was sighted and chased by the 64-gun ship of the line ARDENT; here again the French ship could neither fight nor flee; but as she was not far from the coast, she was run ashore near Cape Finisterre and burnt by her crew. Thus sadly ended the sad story.

8

Successful Defeat

In February 1805 the frigate CLEOPATRA, 32 guns, 12-pounders, Captain Sir Robert Laurie, Bart., was homeward bound from the West Indies. By this time the 32-gun frigates were considered obsolete, and the very last of them was on the stocks, to complete the last order; henceforward there were to be no frigates which did not mount a main battery of 18-pounders at least. To compensate for her now insufficient fire-power, her four quarter-deck 6-pounders had been removed and replaced with ten 24-pounder carronades, bringing her broadside up from 174 pounds to 282; always supposing, of course, that she could get within carronade range. She sailed very well, however, and with her excellent captain and efficient crew could expect to overhaul most enemy ships; she was a little short-handed, having only 200 men and boys instead of her establishment of 214, and she had several of her men down sick with the usual diseases inevitable at that time during a West Indies cruise.

On the 16th of February she was about 250 miles southwest of Bermuda, on the edge of the Sargasso weed, and still in the justly feared Bermuda triangle, the angles of which rest on Bermuda, Florida and Puerto Rico; an area in which more ships have been lost without trace than any other in the world. Not only in the eighteenth century: it has been stated that in the middle of the twentieth century nearly a thousand lives have been lost in this triangle, all without trace. Various theories have been propounded, from frightful monsters emerging from under the Sargasso weed (where, incidentally, all the eels of the Atlantic world go to breed) to the sounder one that, in that sector of a revolving storm in which the hurricane winds were opposed to the current of the Gulf Stream, such a sea would be raised as would overwhelm almost any small ship. Quite probable; but it does not explain the loss, in 1945, of five U.S. Navy torpedo bombers, and of the air-sea rescue ship which went out to look for them; all fitted with radio, all lost without word or trace.

On the 28th January 1805 the French 40-gun 18-pounder frigate *Ville-de-Milan*, Captain Jean-Marie Renaud, sailed from Martinique for France with important despatches, and with strict orders to speak no vessel by the way. To emphasise this stand-offish attitude, her four 36-pounder carronades were removed, and replaced by eight 8-pounder long guns, giving her four long 8s on her forecastle and sixteen on her quarter-deck; to compensate for the extra weight aft, her two after-most 18-pounders were removed, leaving her with a main battery of twenty-six 18-pounders, and twenty 8-pounders, sixteen of which could be traversed to act as stern-chasers; an admirable arrangement for enabling her to carry out her present orders. She was a large frigate of nearly 1,100 tons, with a crew of 350 and a broadside of 340 pounds, all long guns.

It was at dawn on the 16th February that the CLEOPATRA sighted the *Ville-de-Milan* in the south-east, the wind being north-west, and bore up to speak her. By noon it could be descried that she was a large frigate with fifteen broadside ports to her main deck, indicating the 40-gun rate, so that the CLEOPATRA was chasing a ship which must have at least half as much force again as she had. Many a captain in such circumstances would remember a pressing engagement elsewhere, especially if he had reason to believe that the opponent was speedier. A prudent captain would shadow the bigger ship right across the Atlantic, if necessary, in the hope that some other British ship might come in sight to swing the balance of strength the other way; a possibility which would increase the nearer they came to the blockaded shores of France. Sir Robert Laurie, however, was more noted for courage than caution, and his order was to make more sail in pursuit. To the surprise and elation of his officers and crew, who did not know the French captain's orders, the *Ville-de-Milan* also made more sail and positively ran away. More and more sail was spread in both ships, studding-sails were boomed out, and they both tore along under every rag they could carry. Before dark it appeared that the CLEOPATRA was gaining. On both ships studding-sails were carried all night, somewhat hazardously in that area, where sudden squalls such as might dismast an over-pressed ship were quite frequent.

Daylight on the 17th February showed the two ships within four miles of each other, the CLEOPATRA still gaining. By 10.30 a.m. it was clear to Captain Renaud that in spite of his serious attempt to carry out his orders, his audacious opponent was going to bring him to action, so he took in his studding-sails to wait for her. When within gun-shot the CLEOPATRA also took in her studding-sails, and both ships hauled up their main-courses in preparation for action. At noon, observation on board the CLEOPATRA showed that they had chased 180 miles since sighting. At this time, being about half a mile behind, the CLEOPATRA fired her bow-chasers, two long 6-pounders; but the heavy fire returned from the powerful stern-battery of the *Ville-de-Milan* quickly caused her to steer clear, trying to approach the quarter rather than continue a direct stern-chase.

The CLEOPATRA was within a hundred yards at 2.30 p.m., when the *Ville-de-Milan* luffed up close to the wind and gave her opponent two broadsides. The CLEOPATRA closed to within fifty yards before replying, when a furious cannonade commenced and was kept up without intermission all afternoon, while the wind grew stronger and a heavy sea arose. By 5 p.m. both ships had suffered severely, but the rigging of the CLEOPATRA was so much shot about that her sails could scarcely be managed. She now tried to cross her opponent's bow, in the hope of raking her, but while doing so a shot struck her wheel and completely jammed the rudder. The *Ville-de-Milan* was to windward and squaring her sails, she ran right down on the CLEOPATRA, with such force that her bow actually mounted the quarter-deck just aft of the main mast, and she lay with her head and bowsprit right athwart her opponent; from which favourable position she poured in a heavy fire of musketry from her forecastle and fighting tops, to cover an attempt at boarding. This was gallantly repulsed, and the crew of the CLEOPATRA tried to set some sail on her, in the hope of disengaging somehow from the big ship which was pressing her into the sea; but the continuous musketry at so short a range was too much for them. At 5.15 p.m. the *Ville-de-Milan* boarded again, and all resistance ceased.

The fury of the cannonade, and the resolution with which it was continued on both sides, is demonstrated by the damage and casualties. Almost immediately after she was boarded for the second time, the CLEOPATRA lost her foremast, mainmast and bowsprit; and during the night the mainmast and mizzenmast of the *Ville-de-Milan* went overside. Out of a complement of rather less than 200, the CLEOPATRA had fifty-eight killed and wounded, including all her commissioned officers except the captain, her sailing-master and her boatswain. The loss of the *Ville-de-Milan*, out of a crew of 350, has not been definitely ascertained, but was probably about thirty killed and wounded, including, however, her Captain Renaud killed, nearly at the close of the engagement, and her second captain, Capitaine de frégate Pierre Guillet, wounded.

Captain Guillet managed to get the two ships detached, and they lay alongside each other for three days, while a prize crew of fifty officers and men was put on board the *Cleopatra*, a number of the prisoners transferred to the *Ville-de-Milan*, damage was patched, jury-masts rigged and rigging repaired. All this was not helped by the dirty, squally, weather, but by the 21st February the two ships were able to get under way, however slowly.

The 50-gun two-decker LEANDER had had a somewhat chequered career since the Battle of the Nile; under command of Captain John Talbot she was making her way towards the North America station. On the 23rd February, at noon, in a clear spell between squalls, she espied a sail in the distance, to the south, and made sail in chase, losing sight very shortly but continuing on the same course. At 2.30 p.m. the weather cleared, and the chase was made out to be a frigate, jury-rigged; and shortly a much larger ship was seen ahead of her, also under jury masts. They closed, apparently for mutual support, and hoisted French colours. These were, of course, the *Ville-de-Milan* and the *Cleopatra*, neither in any state for another battle. At 4 p.m. the LEANDER came up within gun-shot, when the two frigates separated, the *Cleopatra* running before the wind (she was in no condition to do anything else) and the *Ville-de-Milan* hauling up to take the wind on her quarter, which was about the nearest to the wind she could manage. The LEANDER followed the *Cleopatra*, overtook her in half an hour, and gave her one shot from her 32-pound lower battery; whereupon she hauled down her French colours and lay-to.

Those of the British prisoners who had been left on board now came on deck to take over the ship again, and hailed Captain Talbot to inform him what was happening; he ordered them to follow him as best they could, and immediately went off in pursuit of the *Ville-de-Milan*. The presence of a sufficient British crew was a very fortunate circumstance, as otherwise two hours would have been lost in putting a prize crew on board. As it was, by 5.30 p.m. the LEANDER was alongside the *Ville-de-Milan*, which surrendered without a shot being fired. After providing prize crews and arranging for the security of the prisoners, the LEANDER conducted her prizes into Halifax, where they were thoroughly repaired. The larger was taken into the Royal Navy as the 38-gun frigate MILAN, and the command was, very properly, given to Sir Robert Laurie.

Had the *Ville-de-Milan* met the LEANDER without first fighting the CLEOPATRA, two courses were open to her: no doubt, in accordance with her orders, she would have sailed away, as she was very well able to do, being much faster than the clumsy old two-decker; but had her captain so wished, she might have fought with about equal chances, being somewhat larger in tonnage, more numerously manned, and only slightly lighter in weight of metal, while being much more nimble in manœuvre. However, the hammering she had taken from the CLEOPATRA precluded all thought either of flight or of resistance, and her captain was absolutely correct in surrendering immediately. Sir Robert Laurie, therefore, while he had incurred heavy casualties and temporarily lost his ship, had nevertheless inflicted such damage to his opponent that she was bound to fall a prey to almost any well-found frigate which might encounter her, and this was accomplished only by the bold chase and intrepid encounter with a ship so much superior in every category. This was the sort of engagement Nelson had in mind, when with six ships he went in search of a fleet reported from seventeen to twenty. He assured Earl St Vincent that none of his ships would surrender, 'And before we are destroyed, I have little doubt but they will have their wings so completely clipped, that they may be easily overtaken.' Laurie never had the opportunity to command great fleets like Nelson, but he had the same ideas.

Prospective Admirals, however, will note that the 'successful defeat' went out with the wooden walls. The very last instance of a weak fleet successfully attacking a stronger was the Battle of Lissa in 1866; but there the weak Austrian fleet was commanded by Tegetthof, one of the finest naval officers ever, while the strong Italian fleet was under an officer whose conduct can only with charity be called irresolute. Ever since then, any naval encounter which was pushed home resulted in the destruction of the weaker with negligible damage to the stronger: there is no place in modern warfare for facile optimism.

9

The Young Star-captains

'Where the fleet of stars is anchored, and the young star-captains glow.'

Samuel Pepys laid down excellent rules for promotion in the Royal Navy: an aspirant to a lieutenant's commission had to have had at least six years at sea, been a midshipman or master's mate, and must be examined by a Board of three post captains; once commissioned, his further promotion to commander and captain depended on the view taken by his seniors; once he was captain, nobody could possibly be promoted over his head; only seniority mattered. No doubt if Pepys had exercised his authority for a century or so, things would have been better, but the rules became sadly bent during the eighteenth century. Some sort of influence, or interest as it was then called, was necessary even to get a captain to take a boy on board his ship at all, and from then on influence counted far more than ability. It was especially necessary to get the young man made post captain as early as possible, so that he might attain flag rank before he was *too* senile, and for this end influential persons got the rules broken with complete impunity. Especially was this the case on distant stations, where the Admiral C-in-C could appoint post captains at his discretion, subject always to confirmation by the Board of Admiralty. Thus Admiral Rodney made his son a post captain at sixteen, and Admiral Parker made *his* at seventeen, and both appointments were confirmed by the Board; but neither of them attained any subsequent distinction of his own.

Had Sir John Suckling not been Comptroller of the Navy, it is very unlikely that his nephew Horatio Nelson would have become post captain at twenty, and consequently rear-admiral at thirty-eight, qualified by seniority to command fleets. Of course, the whole system of eighteenth-century patronage was modified by the fact that people of great influence preferred to use it on behalf of youngsters who were likely to do them credit. Moreover, although a captain must inevitably advance by years alone in rank, this did not mean that he *must* have a command. Even when the Navy was at its most numerous in ships, not much more than a third of the captains commanded one; the rest were ashore on half pay. Thus at the beginning of 1811 the active list included 181 flag officers and 753 post captains, but there were only 264 post ships in commission, from 120 guns to 20 guns. And although the Board could be very obliging in allowing an early *rank* to the favoured of 'interest', *command* was a different thing, decided much more by the professional officers of the Board than the political. Where the choice was between two officers of more or less equal suitability, influence might swing the scale; but it would never get an incompetent officer appointed to an important command.

Thomas Byam Martin had dedicated himself to the Navy since early boyhood; not surprisingly, for his father, Sir Henry Martin, was Commissioner for Portsmouth in 1780, and Comptroller of the Navy in 1790. When he first went to sea, at the age of thirteen, it was in the PEGASUS, Captain Prince William Henry, afterwards King William IV. There was no difficulty about his examination and commission as lieutenant, which he received when he was seventeen; and when the great wars began in 1793, he served in the great fleet at Toulon, under the eye of Vice-Admiral Lord Hood.

The Republic of Genoa was of importance in this part of the Mediterranean, occupying 150 miles of strategic coastline, difficult of access from the rest of Italy. Theoretically it was neutral, but there was evidence that its many harbours were in fact being used as bases by French warships. On 5th October 1793 the BEDFORD, 74, Captain Mann, with the CAPTAIN, Captain Reeve, went into the harbour of Genoa itself, and took out the French 36-gun frigate *Modeste*, after a token resistance. On rejoining the fleet off Toulon, Admiral Hood took the frigate into the Royal Navy under its existing name, and made Byam Martin post captain in command of her; he was now twenty years of age.

On the 8th of June 1796 two British frigates were on patrol about fifty miles west of the Scilly Islands. They were the 32-gun 18-pounder UNICORN, and the 36-gun 12-pounder SANTA MARGARITA, Captains Thomas Williams and Thomas Byam Martin respectively. At dawn they saw three strange warships to the south, only three miles away, and made after them. They turned out to be two frigates and a ship-corvette, keeping close together for mutual support. Shortly after noon the frigates hoisted French colours and opened fire with their stern-chasers, doing some damage to the rigging of the pursuers. At 4 p.m. the smaller frigate bore away from the heavy fire of the UNICORN, and cut across the bows of the SANTA MARGARITA, intending to rake her with a broadside; but Captain Byam Martin very neatly evaded this by running alongside his opponent and engaging her in a fierce cannonade broadside to broadside. Twenty minutes of this was enough, and the French captain hauled down his colours, having had 32 killed and 19 badly wounded, against the British loss of 2 killed and 3 wounded. Captain Byam Martin was very pleased to find that his prize was the *Tamise*, formerly the British THAMES, which had been captured in October 1793, after a desperate action with the *Uranie*, of almost twice her force; they fought each other to a standstill, the *Uranie* made off, but three more French frigates came up and took the crippled THAMES.

Meanwhile the UNICORN was in pursuit of the larger opponent, which turned out to be the *Tribune*, a large 36-gun frigate actually mounting 44 guns. After a running fight of ten hours, and a total chase of more than 200 miles, Captain Williams got to close quarters, dismasted his opponent and forced her surrender. She was rather larger than the UNICORN, but the extraordinary thing about this engagement is that while she had thirty-seven men killed and fifteen wounded including her captain, the UNICORN had not a single casualty.

On returning to port, both the first lieutenants of the two frigates were promoted commander, and Captain Williams, the senior captain, was knighted. At twenty-three, Byam Martin could afford to wait.

The TRIBUNE was wrecked the next year, through the folly of her captain and sailing master in trying to enter Halifax, Nova Scotia without a pilot. The THAMES, however, had quite an extensive service after she was restored to the Royal Navy.

In 1797 Byam Martin was given the 38-gun frigate TAMAR, and sent to the West Indies to join the squadron under Rear-Admiral Henry Harvey in the PRINCE OF WALES, 98, with Captain John Harvey as flag captain. (The Harvey family supplied more officers to the Royal Navy than any other at this time, and never a bad one; they, like everybody else, used family interest to the utmost.) The squadron was based on Port Royal, Martinique, which had been taken from the French, and the first objective was Trinidad. The protecting Spanish squadron, four ships of the line and a frigate, were found at anchor in Chaguarama Bay, in a strong position covered by the fortified island of Gaspar Grande. Although he had one ship of the line more than the Spaniards, Harvey also had the responsibility of a fleet of transports with a small army under the famous Lieutenant-General Sir Ralph Abercrombie; evening was coming on, and Harvey decided that nothing was to be lost by waiting until morning. Nor was it: during the night the Spaniards set all their ships on fire except one, and abandoned them, along with the batteries on the island; no doubt they mistook some of the transports for ships of war, and concluded that they were faced with an overwhelming force. The remaining ship, the *San Damiso*, was boarded from the boats of the British ships and taken out without resistance. On the same day the troops were landed near Port of Spain, the capital, which was entered unopposed, and the following day the Spanish governor surrendered the whole island. The total casualties on both sides was one British Army lieutenant wounded.

The next island attempted was Puerto Rico, where the squadron anchored off Boca de Congregos. They were hampered by the lack of detailed charts of that reef-lined shore, but eventually a passage was discovered which allowed sloops or smaller to reach the shore, where the army was disembarked about fifteen miles east of San Juan, not without some opposition. From here they had to advance along the narrow peninsula on the tip of which stood the town, against the strong fortifications which had been erected, and under fire from both sides by light gunboats; while even the lighter ships of the squadron could not, on account of the reefs, get within a distance to give supporting fire. After ten or twelve days spent in trying everything which might occur to so able a General, Sir Ralph withdrew and reembarked, having suffered a heavy loss of 225 killed, wounded and missing.

While all this was excellent experience, and service performed to the satisfaction of his superior officers, there was not much honour and glory to be won as a frigate attending on a line-of-battle squadron whose task was convoying small armies about the West Indies; and Byam Martin was no doubt delighted when his next command, in 1798, was a practically independent one, cruising about in the chops of the Channel looking out for French vessels going to Ireland or, more rarely, going home. In spite of the requirements of the Egyptian expedition under General Buonaparte, the Directory still looked to Ireland as the weak spot in British defence, as was indeed the case; but as in every case in which France tried to stir up rebellion, the aid they sent was too little and too late. The idea in this case was to arm and organise the Irish peasantry (who had good reason to rebel), and support them with a brigade of four or five thousand regular troops, again under General Humbert; a smaller scheme than that of December 1796, but for that reason more feasible. Everything happened, but at the wrong time. In May, Father Murphy had thirty thousand armed peasants assembled; but there was no backbone of French regulars, and they were cut to pieces by General Lake's troops. The first part of the French expedition did not sail from Rochefort until the 6th of August, with General Humbert and about 1,200 men, whom they put on shore in the Bay of Killala and left to their own devices. After about a fortnight of desultory skirmishing, the remnant surrendered at Ballinamuck to General Lake, on 8th September. On the 15th the rest of the army sailed from Brest, at least 3,000 strong, in a 74 and eight frigates, too late for their friends in Ireland, but just in good time for the equinoctial gales. They were sighted by the frigates as they left Brest, and shadowed all the way to the northwest coast of Ireland, while a squadron was being collected to deal with them; this they did so effectively that the 74 and three frigates surrendered in Donegal Bay, while the other five saved themselves for the time by scattering, not a single soldier having been landed.

Captain Byam Martin's frigate was the FISGARD, formerly the French *Résistance*, captured off Brest after the odd expedition to Fishguard (Chapter 4). She was at the top of the 38-gun class, mounting thirty-eight long 18-pounders on the main battery, and eight carronades, 32-pounders, on quarter-deck and forecastle. At 1,182 tons she was one of the largest British frigates, well able to carry her armament and her complement of 284 men, a well-trained crew with a keen and efficient young captain.

It was at 8 a.m. on the 20th of October 1798 that the look-out hailed the deck with the long-hoped-for report—a strange sail to the westward headed directly for Brest, about a hundred miles away, with a fine steady wind from west by south-west. The FISGARD kept on close-hauled for half an hour, then tacked in chase, with the wind nicely on her quarter. The chase was the *Immortalité*, smaller than the FISGARD but slightly more heavily armed, having twenty-four long 24-pounders on her main battery, and fourteen long 8-pounders and four carronades, 36-pounders, on her forecastle and quarter-deck. In addition to her normal complement of 330 men, she had on board 250 soldiers whom she had been unable to land in Ireland.

At 11 a.m. the *Immortalité* hoisted her colours and began firing her long 8-pounder stern-chasers, to which the FISGARD could make no effective return, having only carronades on her forecastle, with the result that when she did come up with her antagonist, she was badly knocked about in the rigging, so much so that after a short engagement she had to fall back to make repairs. On this, the *Immortalité* hoisted all sail and made off on the fair wind. It is easy to imagine the scene of furious activity on the deck of the FISGARD as they saw their enemy escaping; they re-rigged almost the whole ship in three-quarters of an hour, a feat only possible for the very best of crews, most skilfully commanded. By 1.30 p.m. she was again level with the *Immortalité*, keeping wide during the chase to avoid that battery of stern-chasers, and then converging, but keeping far enough away to be out of range of aimed musketry from the 250 soldiers. Now ensued a most furious cannonade, both sides standing to their guns with the utmost resolution. The FISGARD

received some of her opponent's heavy 24-pound shot between wind and water, and at 2 p.m. the carpenter reported
six feet of water in the hold. He was ordered to keep plugging
and pumping, and the cannonade went on for another hour
with undiminished fury. By this time the hull of the *Immortalité* was in a sinking condition, her mizzen-mast gone by the
board, and the rest of her masts very badly damaged; moreover, her gallant Captain Legrand and the first lieutenant were
both killed, as also General Monge of the Army; she now
hauled down her colours and surrendered.

The FISGARD had thirty-six killed and wounded, and her hull
so damaged that after all possible repairs she had to keep one
pump going continually all the way to Plymouth. The *Immortalité* had 115 killed and wounded, including the officers mentioned. This was a classic example of a combat between two
ships well matched in force, meeting on the high seas with
plenty of sea-room and no other ship in sight the whole day.
The hard-fought fight was equally honourable to both com-
batants, but of course the laurels go to the victor. The IMMOR-
TALITE was taken into the Royal Navy under her own name,
but after the hammering she had taken from the FISGARD she
was reckoned not strong enough to remount 24-pounders, which
were replaced by 18s.

This was the last of Byam Martin's exploits as a frigate captain; henceforth he commanded ships of the line during the
rest of the wars, always with credit and success. He became
Admiral of the Fleet in 1849, and died, full of years and
honours, in 1854.

The East Indies station was the command that gave the wid-
est powers and discretion to the C-in-C, because of the great
distance. To send a despatch from Fort St George to London
by the usual convoy, with long stops at the Cape of Good Hope
and St Helena, took about six months, so that a reply could not
be looked for inside a year; and unless the despatch from Admiralty was very peremptory, another year might well elapse
before the C-in-C had to alter his plans. In fact this scarcely
ever happened; the C-in-C was always a proved and trusted
officer, Admiralty gave him a broad picture of what was expected, and left the details to him; that he would promote his
relatives was taken for granted, within reasonable limits. Thus
when Rear-Admiral Peter Rainier as C-in-C, East Indies

station, made an expedition under his own command to take Amboyna, it is not surprising to find James Sprat Rainier in command of the 16-gun ship-sloop SWIFT, in February 1796; nor is it surprising that in 1799 he was a post captain in command of the two-decker 50-gun ship CENTURION, in the Mediterranean; but on the renewal of the war in 1803 he was back on the East Indies station, in the same ship. He never commanded a frigate.

Now Vice-Admiral, Rainier had his nephew and godson, Midshipman Peter Rainier, sent out to the East Indies, and in very little more than a year made him post captain in the 36-gun 18-pounder frigate CAROLINE; quick promotion, but it had to be quick, for Rear-Admiral Sir Edward Pellew was already on his way to relieve Rainier, and he had with him his son, Fleetwood Pellew, whom he had already had made a commander at seventeen. He might possibly not have observed those qualities in young Rainier which his uncle did, but now that Peter junior was a post captain there was nothing to be done about it. In fact, Pellew did very well by Rainier's protégé, and sent him out on very promising cruises.

On the 18th of October 1806 the CAROLINE captured a small 14-gun Dutch brig, off the north coast of Java; and learned from the prisoners that there was a Dutch 36-gun 12-pounder frigate, the *Maria-Riggersbergen*, in the roadstead at Batavia (now Djakarta). Captain Rainier at once followed up this information, and found not only the frigate but three other ships, two of 14 guns and one of 18, as well as more than thirty gun-boats close inshore. Captain Rainier prepared to anchor by the stern, with a spring on the cable, and sailed boldly in; as soon as the CAROLINE was within shot the *Maria-Riggersbergen* opened fire, but the CAROLINE remained quite silent until within forty yards, when she loosed her broadside with devastating effect. The Dutch ship fought back bravely, and had the three smaller ships and the mass of gun-boats come boldly forward, they would have had a superiority of three to one against the CAROLINE; but their efforts were very half-hearted, and within half an hour the *Maria-Riggersbergen* hauled down her colours and the CAROLINE took possession. The CAROLINE was undermanned, having sent away 57 men in various prizes; of the 204 remaining she had 21 killed or wounded, plus 4 Dutch prisoners, and scarcely any damage to the hull or rigging. The Dutch frigate, out of a complement of 270, lost 50 killed or wounded, and had extensive but tolerable damage.

Sir Edward Pellew took the frigate into the Royal Navy, under the more pronounceable name of JAVA. On the East Indies station a ship was a ship, hard to replace, but had she been at Portsmouth she would not have been taken into full service, being fairly old and not in good condition. The following year, under Captain George Pigot, she was escorting in the Indian Ocean the BLENHEIM, 74, wearing the flag of Vice-Admiral Sir Thomas Troubridge, Bart., that most renowned of Nelson's paladins. What actually happened will never be known, for both ships disappeared without a trace. No doubt they had met the full force of a typhoon, which might conceivably have overwhelmed them both without a boat or spar breaking away. It cannot have been very far from the place where the new 12,000 ton liner *Waratah*, fitted with radio, disappeared without signal or trace in 1898.

In January 1807 the CAROLINE, and her young captain, had a stroke of luck such as every man in the Navy liked to dream about. They captured the Spanish *San Raphael*, with trifling resistance, and found her so richly laden that her prize-money came to nearly £170,000. The twenty-two-year-old captain had more than £50,000, while the C-in-C, Pellew, thousands of miles away, had half that sum; still, there was cut-and-come-again left, and the most ordinary seaman had about £200, enough to set him up in a cosy pub on shore, while the lieutenants would have more than £5,000 apiece. The timing was lucky too; had the capture taken place eighteen months later, the CAROLINE would have found, on reaching port, that Spain was now Britain's gallant ally and there was no prize-money forthcoming.

Rear-Admiral Sir Edward Pellew had lost no time in making his son Fleetwood Pellew, age twenty, a post captain in the 32-gun 12-pounder PSYCHE; he now sent the two young captains out together on a long-range reconnaissance. It was known that there were two Dutch ships of the line, 68 guns each, somewhere on the Java coast. At a time when a very few warships were controlling vast areas of ocean, two powerful warships were of such importance that it was imperative to discover their whereabouts and condition. Accordingly the CAROLINE and the PSYCHE sailed from Fort St George in June

1807, and at the end of August reached the eastern end of Java. Here they were able to ascertain that the two Dutch line-ships were the *Pluto* and the *Revolutie*, that they were laid up in Gressik at the mouth of the Sourabaya river, unfit to go to sea and probably in too poor a condition to be repairable.

This meant that there was most probably no ship in the area which could be a match for either of the frigates separately; accordingly they parted, the CAROLINE sailing back by the south side of Java and the PSYCHE by the northern. When off Samarang, about 200 miles west of Sourabaya, shipping was observed in the roadstead towards evening, and the PSYCHE anchored offshore for the night. At dawn she stood into the harbour and found a small 8-gun schooner and a merchant brig, which were seized and towed out by the boats of the frigate, under Lieutenant Kersteman. Now three more vessels appearing to be warships were seen in the offing; Captain Fleetwood Pellew therefore destroyed his prizes, not wishing to weaken his crew by detaching prize-crews. On making sail in pursuit of the strangers, they made off to the westward, but finding that the frigate was quickly overtaking them they ran themselves on shore. In this position they opened fire on the frigate, trusting to the shallows to keep her at a distance, while they could probably deal with the boats if sent in. The PSYCHE, however, ghosted in until she anchored with scarcely half a yard of water beneath her keel; from here she fired broadsides at each of the three in turn, and in about an hour all three struck their colours. They were the *Revolutie*, an armed merchantman of 700 tons, the 24-gun corvette *Scipio*, and the 12-gun brig *Ceres*. They had very little damage and the only casualty was the Captain of the *Scipio* killed; the PSYCHE had no damage or casualties. By working hard all through the night, the crew of the PSYCHE got all three prizes floated off, and brought them to Madras.

It may seem strange that such great ship-builders as the Dutch should allow their two best ships to fall into hopeless disrepair, and that such determined fighters should so tamely surrender their ships; whereas in the first war the Dutch were considered the toughest of opponents, and Camperdown was by far the most desperately contested battle of the wars. The fact is that their hearts were no longer in it. When the Batavian Republic was in alliance with the French Republic they fought with a right good will; but when the Kingdom of Holland was a vassal state of the French Empire, with a Louis Buonaparte on the throne, their enthusiasm evaporated. In all war it is essential that men 'should know what they fight for, and like what they know'.

Before long Sir Edward promoted his son to the command of the 38-gun 18-pounder frigate PHAETON, in which ship he remained on the station after his father returned to take over the Mediterranean command on the death of Admiral Collingwood. In this ship he served in the powerful fleet under Rear-Admiral Stopford which, along with 10,000 troops, finally took all Java in 1811. The naval force of four line-of-battle ships, fourteen frigates, and many smaller craft, was so great that there was no resistance by sea; but Captain Fleetwood Pellew saw some service on land, in command of about a hundred men.

Unlike Byam Martin, neither Rainier nor Pellew further distinguished themselves. Rainier commanded several ships at different times, but was never involved in any famous action. Pellew had great difficulty in getting a command at all. Although certainly a brave and efficient officer, he had acquired such an unfortunate reputation for brutality towards his crew that it was difficult to get anybody to serve under him, and he was always having near-mutinies, which were sometimes quite serious. After he had been on the beach for many years, having attained flag rank by simple survival, he was given command of the squadron which went out in 1842 to take over Hong Kong. Even here he managed to have a mutiny by refusing to allow shore leave to the crews, owing, he alleged, to the bad and dangerous climate. The ship which took home his despatches brought back another admiral to relieve him.

10

The Last Viking

Excepting Nelson, no naval officer impressed himself so much upon his times, as a hero of romance, as Captain Lord Cochrane. Certainly he had every advantage. Eldest son of the Scottish Earl of Dundonald, he was very tall, immensely strong, and of a most imposing presence, even as a very young man. He had every good quality of the warrior, leaving nothing to chance but accepting ascertained risks, absolutely without fear but retaining his cool head in the midst of the fiercest combat. He trained his men in the same strict discipline that he trained himself, and they loved him. He was strictly impartial: for example, it was absolutely necessary that every man should roll up his hammock very tightly before stowing it in the hammock nettings above the bulwarks; Cochrane had an iron hoop made, and every hammock, when rolled, had to pass through the hoop, or else. There was no room for the whim of a boatswain's mate; either the hammock passed the hoop or it didn't. When he came to the command of ships, he had never the least difficulty in getting together a crew, the only trouble being in selecting from the over-numerous volunteers. In his official letters, he never mentioned his own part, but lavished praise on his officers and men, who no doubt deserved it because they had absorbed his own high spirit, as had Nelson's officers.

Nevertheless, he had the defects of his qualities. He could not see any injustice or abuse without attacking it with the same headlong ardour that he did the French; but alas! the shining knight was unhorsed by the windmills. The whole Establishment of the time—religious, civil, Army or Navy, was completely based on the great principles of patronage and corruption, and woe betide the solitary stormer of those bastions! Cochrane himself was quite illegally enrolled on the books of the various ships commanded by his uncle, from the time he was five years old until he actually went on board a warship for the first time at the age of eighteen; this to give him a sufficient 'sea-time' to qualify him to sit the examination for lieutenant. This sort of cheating and exercise of influence was absolutely necessary if a young man was to get his foot on the captain's ladder when young enough to give him a chance of becoming at least a rear-admiral before he was too old for active service, but it was a bad way to officer a navy.

In December 1801 Cochrane was made a post captain, and might reasonably expect command of a frigate. He had the right connections and a splendid record; in his last cruise, in a very small brig, he had terrorised the Mediterranean coast of Spain, capturing 50 ships, 122 guns and 534 prisoners, and conducted the most brilliant single-ship encounter in naval history. When he was made post, he urged the claim of his first lieutenant to be promoted commander for this last exploit; when refused, he returned again, pressing his point in terms which were certainly undiplomatic, and which the First Sea Lord, Earl St Vincent, took as personally insulting. The grim old admiral never forgave; there was no ship for Cochrane to command; the most brilliant of the young captains was on the beach.

On the resumption of war after the brief Peace of Amiens, in 1803, Cochrane again offered his services, and was given the ARAB, an old coal boat which had been fitted with just enough guns to qualify as a post-ship, and detailed for coastal duties in the Channel, west of Beachy Head, as part of the protection against Napoleon's army gathered at Boulogne for the invasion. Not much of a command for an active officer, but the country was in quite a fever of apprehension (with some cause), for if Napoleon had set down in Kent the army which he later led to Austerlitz, there was very little in Britain to match that superbly equipped and trained force. The only problem was getting them to Kent, and St Vincent spoke for the Navy when he told the House of Lords, 'I do not say the French cannot come, but I do say they cannot come by water.'

In May 1804 the Addington Cabinet fell, and Pitt became Prime Minister, with his friend Henry Dundas, now made

Viscount Melville, as First Lord of the Admiralty. This active Scotsman introduced a great programme of naval expansion, in which he was unlikely to overlook another active Scotsman. Cochrane got his frigate, the 32-gun PALLAS, 667 tons, newly built of fir instead of oak, with a main battery of twenty-six long 12-pounders and twelve carronades, 24-pounders, on her quarter-deck and forecastle. No doubt many captains junior to Cochrane commanded much more powerful ships; still, it was a frigate, fast by reason of its light structure, and fitted for its intended role of raiding commerce and inshore patrol. Moreover, he was given a very desirable commission; to proceed under Admiralty letter to the vicinity of the Azores, and cruise there for enemy merchantmen, which meant that all the prize-money would fall to the ship's company, without deductions for distant admirals or other senior officers. After a certain time in this employment, he was to proceed to the Biscay coast of France and put himself under the orders of Vice-Admiral Thornborough, commanding in that area.

The Azores cruise was highly profitable, and after seeing his prizes safely into Gibraltar, Cochrane went to the Biscay station. Hanging about off the Gironde, the estuary which leads up to Bordeaux, he found out that the entrance was guarded by two 14-gun brig-corvettes, taking turn about up-river and down-river, the estuary being further defended by land batteries on both shores. Cochrane could see no good reason why he should not have at least one of those brigs, and on the evening of 5th April 1806 he sent in all the boats of the frigate, under the command of his first lieutenant, John Hansell, and piloted by his sailing master James Sutherland, the other boats being commanded by three midshipmen; the PALLAS anchored to await their return, and to prevent any interference from outside. Even with the help of the tide it was a long pull of twenty miles for the men, but by 3 a.m. on the morning of the 6th they were alongside, and boarded her in great style. There was no surprise, for the brig was fully prepared, but nothing could resist the men Cochrane had trained, and in a few minutes the brig, the *Tapageuse*, was their prize. They now looked to the other brig, further up-stream, but the tide had turned and there were not enough men to look after the *Tapageuse*, whose crew outnumbered the PALLAS boatmen, and attack her consort also; so, at first light they made sail outwards. Immediately the shore guards gathered what was happening, the batteries opened fire on the TAPAGEUSE, and the other brig made sail in pursuit, coming within gunshot and engaging in a desultory exchange of long bowls for about an hour, when the sight of the three masts of the PALLAS persuaded them to desist. The whole loss in this engagement, a class-room demonstration of 'cutting out by boats' was three men wounded.

The PALLAS had not been swinging idly at her anchor. At dawn she was under way, having seen three ships approaching, which were in fact the two 20-gun ship-corvettes *Garonne* and *Gloire*, and the 16-gun brig-corvette *Malicieuse*. Between them those ships mounted 56 guns to the 38 of the PALLAS, but they showed no desire to engage. The PALLAS ran all three of them ashore, where they were all dismasted by the shock of striking, and lay, apparently, complete wrecks. Had they been well handled, they could very well have given a good account of themselves, especially as so many men of the PALLAS were away in the boats; this of course they could not know, but what they probably did know was the name of the frigate, and who commanded her, and the terror of his name. Having seen the three Frenchmen ashore, the PALLAS returned to her station in good time to receive her boats and their prize.

After re-uniting with Vice-Admiral Thornborough's squadron, the PALLAS was detached on 25th April 1806 to reconnoitre the Aix roads, between the Île d'Oleron and the mainland at Rochefort, the heavily fortified Île d'Aix lying in the centre of the northern end of the roadstead, about 46°N 1°10′W. Standing boldly in, Lord Cochrane observed one three-decker and four two-decked line-of-battle ships, five frigates, a ship-corvette and three brig-corvettes. Not being in any particular hurry, Cochrane hung about for a while in the roadstead, in case there might be any more information, and to see what might turn up. Signals were seen from the three-decker; and one frigate, the 40-gun *Minerve*, with the three brig-corvettes, weighed and got under way to drive the PALLAS away. Not wishing to hurry, Cochrane waited for the French ships, and, as they approached exchanged several broadsides with them, without, apparently, any damage or casualties. There now were visible the 32-gun 12-pounder frigate IRIS, the 16-gun ship-sloop HAZARD, and a cutter; so that Captain Collet of the

Minerve judged it prudent to take his little squadron under the batteries of Île d'Aix. As he showed no signs of coming out, and as it was inadvisable to engage the whole French fleet in the roads, Cochrane rejoined his squadron to make his report.

Napoleon had instituted a system of coastal signal stations, all within easy view of each other, and also communicating with Paris; by this means every movement of the British inshore cruisers was almost instantly known all along the coast, and this knowledge saved many merchant ships which must otherwise have been snapped up, whereas they simply remained in a fortified anchorage until the coast was clear. These signal posts were quite large structures, with barracks and other buildings, guarded by from fifty to a hundred militia. Having a few days to spare, Cochrane decided to make a break in the line, by destroying half a dozen neighbouring stations; this was done by landing parties, who chased away the militia, took off the flags and burned the masts and buildings. For men trained by Cochrane, this was a straightforward job in five cases, but the sixth was more complicated. At L'Aiguillon, on the Breton Strait between the Île de Ré and the mainland, the signal station was guarded to seaward by a battery of three 32-pounder guns firing explosive shells, and at the time a small French convoy was lying under the protection of the battery, which had a garrison of fifty regulars. Cochrane led a night attack in person, which was successful. The battery was stormed, the guns spiked, the shells thrown into the sea, the emplacements demolished, the buildings and gun-carriages burnt. Next, the signal station was razed like the others, but there was one disappointment: the convoy, which they had expected to capture, had got up the river Lay into safety.

It was now known that the commanding officer of the French squadron in Aix roads was Vice-Admiral Allemand, and it was thought wise to keep a close eye on so able an officer. Accordingly, on the 12th May 1806 the PALLAS again approached, accompanied by the INDEFATIGABLE, 44 guns, Captain John Rodd, and the KINGFISHER, 16 guns, Commander Seymour. The INDEFATIGABLE, Pellew's old ship, was twice the size and power of the PALLAS, but Cochrane was senior to Rodd. Two frigates and three brigs came out to meet them. There was very little sea-room for eight ships, shoals were numerous, and the wind fell light and variable, so that there was every chance of running aground or being becalmed under one of the batteries. The British squadron withdrew, doubtless reflecting that there would be another day.

It came two days later, the 14th May, when the PALLAS, alone, worked her way in against a fair breeze from south by west, which ensured a good retreat if necessary. The *Minerve* and the three brig-corvettes were again ordered out, but this time the *Minerve* came along in great style, flying before the fresh wind with every stitch set, even to studding-sails and royals, determined to bring the PALLAS to action and eliminate this nuisance once for all; this was not impossible by any means, since she was 1,100 tons to the 667 tons of the PALLAS, and had more than twice her weight of broadside. Lord Cochrane, who had shortened sail to topsails only, set his main topsail aback and lay-to until the *Minerve* came within short range, when he gave her such a broadside as effectually shortened her sail for her.

There ensued a battle unique in naval annals, such as could only be fought by a captain of complete intrepidity and consummate skill, with an enthusiastically devoted ship's company. He was engaged with a ship of twice the power, along with three brigs which had between them more guns than he had; he was always within range of at least one of the shore batteries, on the island of Aix or on the coast; and the battle was fought in a confined strait, further encumbered with many hidden shoals. His tactics were to engage the *Minerve*, and at the same time to keep close to her in such a position that the nearest shore battery could not fire without danger of hitting their own ship; at the same time to fight off the three brigs, with their fourteen 8-pounders apiece, who came swarming in; and, still at the same time, to keep in mind the positions of the shoals and sound continually, for a touch on the ground would be instant disaster. With all those conflicting calls for immediate attention, it was only one of the great captains who could continuously issue his orders, completely imperturbable, amid the thunder of the guns and the scream of the shot.

After two hours of this extraordinary combat, the fire of the *Minerve* perceptibly slackened, and Cochrane determined to board her, for an immediate decision; this was essential, for the look-out reported that two more frigates in the roadstead were hoisting sail. As the PALLAS approached, the fire of the *Minerve* ceased altogether; there seemed to be no preparation to repel boarders, for there was nobody to be seen on deck but Captain Collet and a few officers on the quarter-deck. As the ships came alongside, at some speed, a surge threw them together with great force; and the difference was seen between the light fir timbers of the PALLAS and the stout Adriatic oak of the *Minerve*, which took no injury by the collision. The PALLAS lost her jib-boom, fore-topmast, fore and main topsail yards, all her forward rigging, and all the ship-furniture of her side forward, including her cat-head and bower-anchor, by which Cochrane had intended to hook her on to the *Minerve*. There was no question now of re-engaging, for the two fresh frigates were on their way. Setting what sail she could, the PALLAS made outwards to the offing, where she met the KINGFISHER, sloop, which took her in tow. Cochrane, having fought against fearful odds to within a few minutes of victory, was defeated by the cheeseparing economies of his own government.

Casualties were low for such an engagement. PALLAS had one Marine killed, one midshipman and four ratings wounded. Her damages were such that she had to return to Portsmouth for extensive repair. The *Minerve*, with a much larger crew (330 against 214) reported seven killed and fourteen wounded. She had her fore-yard shot away, and much minor damage, easily repaired in Rochefort. She was certainly at sea on 25th September of the same year, for on that day she was captured, along with three other frigates, by a powerful squadron of six line-of-battle ships under Commodore Sir Samuel Hood, who lost his right arm in the engagement. The French frigates put up a determined resistance against such overwhelming odds, and enabled the *Themis*, 36, and two brigs to escape. The *Minerve*, at last, struck her colours to the MONARCH, 74, and was taken into the Royal Navy under the name of ALCESTE; she will be heard of again.

Cochrane's official letters on those actions were, as usual with him, very terse, describing the engagements very briefly and mentioning many of his officers, without any hint of his own conduct; Vice-Admiral Thornbury, in his despatch, did Cochrane full justice, commending him to the attention of their lordships; but when Cochrane came home no attention whatever was paid to him. His friend Lord Melville had left the Admiralty, to be succeeded by Lord Barham, who in turn was followed by Charles Grey, created Lord Howick, merely a politician and quite new in the office, very unlikely to do anything against the advice of the Establishment at the Admiralty, which persisted in the view that no amount of courage and skill could help an officer who had dared to question the justice of omniscient Admiralty. Although nineteen frigates were added to the Royal Navy during the year 1806, there was none for its best frigate captain.

Unwilling to rust on the beach, Cochrane now got himself elected Member of Parliament for Honiton, in October 1806. In our days, when a back-bench Member of Parliament is merely 'a welfare officer for his constituents',* it is difficult to understand the immense influence wielded by every member who could speak to the point, even if he represented 'a grassy mound in an unpeopled plain' or 'three niches in a wall'.† Feeling that Lord Cochrane's heavy guns would be better directed against the French than against themselves, the Lords of the Admiralty ('their feelings matter not') posted him to the IMPERIEUSE, 38-gun 18-pounder frigate, with orders to join Commodore Keats' squadron in the south of the French Biscay coast.

On the way down the familiar Biscay shore, Cochrane thought he would like to look into the Basin d'Arcachon, about seventy miles south of the entrance to the Gironde estuary. There was, however, a strong fort on Cap Ferret, the point of the peninsula which entirely protects the land-locked basin. To clear the way, Cochrane sent all his boats ashore, under Lieutenant David Mapleton, to assault the fort, which looked large and formidable. The men of the IMPERIEUSE, however, stormed the fort and chased away its garrison; then they spiked all the guns, four 36-pounders, two 6-pounder field guns, and a 13-inch mortar for throwing explosive shells. They burned the military stores, platforms and gun-carriages, and used the gunpowder to blow up the buildings. The road into the basin was now open, but it does not appear that there was

* The late Sir James Henderson Stewart, Bt., M.P., in personal conversation with the author.

† Lord John Russel, House of Commons, March 1st 1831, introducing a Reform Bill.

any valuable prize there. Cochrane generally laid his plans so well, and they were carried out with such *élan* that his casualties were generally light; on this occasion there were none whatever. This beautiful little action took place on 6th January 1807.

Cochrane was not long with Commodore Keats' squadron, for Parliament was prorogued on 27th April, and dissolved, with a view to a general election. Cochrane went home, gave up his seat for Honiton, and got himself elected as one of the two members for the City of Westminster. This was unique among constituencies at that time; there was no bribery, and almost every householder was a voter. In those days of pocket boroughs and open bribery, Westminster alone represented *vox populi*—and it was heard. The new Parliament met at the end of May 1807, and on 10th July Cochrane tabled a motion about the scandalous abuses in the Navy, couched in terms which his friends thought injudicious. The motion was never heard in the House. Cochrane was immediately ordered to reassume command of the IMPERIEUSE, proceed to the Mediterranean, and put himself under the orders of Vice-Admiral Lord Collingwood.

Whether Collingwood did not want such a firebrand under his direct command, or whether he thought the service suited to Cochrane's experience and resource, at any rate he detached him with orders to harass the coasts of France and Spain, from Toulon westward as far as Barcelona. This Cochrane pitched into with enthusiasm, first destroying the signal stations which reported his movements, then the batteries under which shipping could lie in safety, and then snapping up prizes all along the coast and sending them in to Minorca. There were few nights without a boating party, and the enemy had to devote more and more troops to guarding the coast and the lines of communication.

In May 1808 there was a change: the population of Spain rose with one accord against the French garrisons which had been allowed into Spain by the treachery of Godoy. The juntas sent deputations to England to ask for help. Help was promised, and the first step was to announce to the Navy that Britain was now at peace with Spain, and that all possible assistance was to be given to the ships and armies of the juntas. Cochrane's role was not much affected, but more complicated; before, he had only to fire at anything that moved; now he had to be selective. However, the disciplined armies which France was now pouring into Spain were readily distinguishable from the guerrillas.

A French army was besieging the frontier fortress of Gerona, and as part of the operation seized a castle and established an outpost on the coastal part of the road between Gerona and Barcelona, thus cutting off supplies to the besieged town. On the 31st July 1808 Lord Cochrane landed with his Marines, stormed the castle and demolished it with all its outworks, taking seventy-one prisoners. He gave all their arms to the guerrillas, but judged it more humane to take the prisoners off in the IMPERIEUSE.

To facilitate the movement of his armies into Spain, Napoleon had erected a chain of signal stations, not with flags as on the west coast but with semaphores after the British pattern, the advantage being that they did not depend upon the wind to spread the flags. Cochrane was cruising off the coast of Languedoc, and towards the end of September recommenced his attacks on the signal stations. He landed, with a large part of his men, at I   ougnan, surprised and demolished a chain of six signal posts, with all their buildings, a shore battery, and a tower on the shore of the Etange de Thau. This was a most daring enterprise, for it was carried out against garrison forces more than double his own in aggregate, within twenty-five miles of the military centre of Montpellier, and ten miles from the highway down which a hundred thousand men were marching for Spain. It deprived them not only of their communications but of their supplies, for without information the coasting vessels which accompanied the armies scarcely dared venture from harbour, and those which did were promptly snapped up by the IMPERIEUSE. His movements were so swift that the French never knew where to expect him, and his attacks were delivered with such impetuosity that no equal force could stand against him. Eventually, the French had to station ten thousand men along the coast which he menaced, so that the mere terror of his name was as effective as a minor fortress.

The fortress and harbour of Rosas, only twenty miles south of the French border, was stoutly defended by the Spaniards, aided from time to time by two British 74s and two bomb-vessels. On the 7th November 1808 the French occupied the town of Rosas, and began siege operations against the citadel and the detached Fort Trinidad, also erecting batteries to drive away the ships. In this they were partly successful, for by the 24th November the 74s had withdrawn the Marines they had landed, and sailed away, leaving the two bomb-vessels, LUCIFER and METEOR, to carry on shelling the French trenches. On the 24th the IMPERIEUSE came into the bay; it was impossible to get to the citadel, but Fort Trinidad was open to seaward, and Cochrane went ashore himself to ascertain the position. The garrison, only eighty strong, was ready to surrender, but decided to hold out, since Cochrane himself undertook to take part in the defence, with fifty seamen and thirty Marines. The Spaniards were astonished at the energy of the Englishmen, and especially admired Cochrane's resource in filling up the breach in the wall with bags filled with earth and sand; indeed, this is possibly the first time sandbags were used as a protection against artillery and musketry. On the 30th November a force of a thousand first-class French troops made a general assault on the fort; after a determined attack and equally determined defence they were repulsed, with heavy losses including their commanding officer and all their equipment.

On the 5th of December 1808 the citadel of Rosas surrendered by capitulation, after a most creditable defence. There was now no point in defending Fort Trinidad any longer, so during the night Cochrane re-embarked, giving passage to those of the garrison who wished to leave that part of the country. He brought away the lighter stores and guns, spiked the heavy guns, and finally blew up the fort. He had delayed for ten days a French army under Marshal St-Cyr, and he had not lost a man. As usual, his official letter was far too brief, a bare statement of facts, with high praise for all his officers engaged, among whom we may distinguish Midshipman Frederick Marryat.

In February 1809 several squadrons which were blockaded on the west coast of France managed to evade the blockade in bad weather, and gathered together in the Aix roads, under the command of Rear-Admiral Willaumez, who was superseded by Vice-Admiral Allemand. His fleet consisted of nine line-of-battle ships, a cut-down 50-gun ship, and four frigates. His flag-ship was the *Ocean*, 120 guns, one of the most powerful ships afloat. Outside, in the Basque roads, lay Admiral Lord Gambier, with eleven line-of-battle ships, including the new CALEDONIA, 120 guns, a match for the *Ocean*, with six frigates, twelve smaller warships, and a number of store and transport ships. He made excellent dispositions for the defence of his fleet, but none for attacking the enemy. Admiralty could not spare so fine a fleet to lie at anchor close to the enemy shore; neither could they permit so powerful a French fleet to remain within easy reach of the immense convoys which were supplying the British forces in Spain and Portugal: it must be destroyed. On the 19th March Admiralty sent Lord Gambier a despatch, advising him that they were sending to his aid twelve fireships, and Colonel Congreve with a supply of his rockets and men to use them; he was furthermore directed, 'to take into your consideration the possibility of making an attack upon the enemy . . .'. (In short, don't just sit there, *do* something.) In reply, on the 26th March, Lord Gambier wrote a long despatch emphasising the enormous difficulties, for he was a man who always saw his own troubles very clearly, but had no imagination of the difficulties of the enemy; however, he concluded that he was ready to obey any orders, 'however great the risk may be of the loss of men and ships'.

On the 19th March, the same day that the Admiralty sent the prod to Gambier, the IMPERIEUSE, with Lord Cochrane in command, anchored at Plymouth; and it says much for the Admiralty system of semaphores that within an hour he received an order to attend at Whitehall. On the 21st March he was received by Lord Mulgrave, the First Lord, who explained the position in Aix roads and asked him to give his opinion, based on his intimate knowledge of the area, as to whether an attempt would be successful. He thought it had every prospect. Given suitable weather conditions, twelve fireships would cause the utmost confusion, if not panic, and in a confined roadstead, encumbered with shoals, several at least of the big ships must go aground; unable to manœuvre, they could be forced to surrender by a few bomb-ships, some gunbrigs with heavy carronades, and two or three frigates in deeper water. Cochrane was now asked if he himself would take command of such an attack. He refused, on the grounds that there were many officers senior to himself in Lord Gambier's fleet, and his being given such a command over their heads would cause a great deal of ill-feeling. 'The present is no time for professional etiquette,' said Lord Mulgrave, and pointed out that he was the only captain who knew the ground thoroughly, and also was confident that the attempt would succeed; on this Lord Cochrane agreed, as he would not have it thought that he would propose a hazardous attack which he would not undertake in person.

Admiralty now sent an official despatch to Lord Gambier, informing him that they had selected Captain Lord Cochrane to conduct (under Lord Gambier's directions) the attack by fireships and other vessels on the enemy in Aix roads. This despatch was carried by Cochrane himself, who delivered it in person on 3rd April 1809. The social effect was as he expected, although he could not know that Rear-Admiral the Hon. Robert Stopford, second-in-command of the fleet, had proposed just such an attack, had offered to command it himself, and had been turned down by Lord Gambier. Now a young captain had somehow got himself an Admiralty instruction to Gambier to give him the command that Stopford had been refused. However, orders were orders, and the work at once commenced of fitting out fireships, explosion vessels and light rocket-carriers.

Unknown to the British, the fleet assembled in the Aix roads had been intended for the relief of the West Indian island of Martinique, which was hard pressed by a strong fleet under Rear-Admiral Sir Alexander Cochrane, uncle of Captain Lord Cochrane, and an army of ten thousand men under Lieutenant-General Beckwith. However, the news came through that the island had surrendered on the 24th February, and Vice-Admiral Allemand, having no further orders, took all proper steps to make his position in Aix roads secure. He knew the position well: it was very different from the secure harbour of Brest; an open roadstead, beset with reefs and encumbered with shoals; very open to an attack by fireships, or an attack à la Aboukir, had there been a Nelson in command in the blockading fleet. Against the latter possibility, he moored his ships in two parallel lines almost a mile in length, with a distance of rather more than two ships' lengths between each ship, and the two lines staggered, so that each ship was opposite the corresponding space in the other line. This ensured that any ship could engage without danger of firing on one of her consorts. The frigates formed a third line. This excellent disposition ensured that if an enemy fleet entered the roadstead in line ahead—and no other formation was possible —each ship as it advanced would come under the fire of two ships without the danger of their firing into each other. Against bomb vessels he had the heavy shore batteries, which could sink a bomb-ketch with a single hit, also his frigates and brigs. Against fireships, he laid down a great boom, composed of enormous cables more than 30 inches in diameter, secured by five-ton anchors and floated by numerous buoys. This boom was half a mile in length, and completely closed off the channel leading from the Basque roads to the Aix roads. He further ordered that all the boats of the fleet were to patrol the boom from dusk till dawn to drive away any British boats, and to be prepared to board fireships and steer them to shore at a safe distance from the fleet. The ships of the line were ordered to strike all their upper masts and sails, as they were to fight at anchor; but the frigates and smaller vessels were to be in a state of instant readiness to sail as requisite. For a fleet blockaded in an open roadstead by a superior fleet those orders could not be improved upon, and show that Vice-Admiral Allemand was a most able and resourceful officer.

Lord Cochrane's dispositions were made so completely and prudently that he refuted for ever the charge made by his ill-wishers that he was a mere berserker, rushing upon the foe without heed or preparation. His own ship, the IMPERIEUSE, was to anchor just out of gun-shot of the French fleet, with the explosion vessels beside her. Three frigates, AIGLE, UNICORN and PALLAS, were to anchor a little further out, with the fireships. The ETNA, his only bomb-ship, was stationed near the Île d'Aix, to bombard the batteries when they opened fire, and the INDEFATIGABLE, 44-gun frigate, and FOXHOUND, 18-gun sloop, were detailed to cover her. A schooner and two cutters, which had been fitted for discharging Congreve rockets, were stationed near the IMPERIEUSE, to move in with the fireships. A frigate and four smaller vessels were to appear to attempt to pass into the road by the east side of the Île d'Aix. Two small

10-gun sloops, REDPOLE and LYRA, were sent in to show lights, screened from the enemy, to guide in the fireships. The fireships were well prepared, as three French coasters laden with tar and resin had recently been captured, and leading them was the MEDIATOR, Captain James Woolridge, a 32-gun frigate which had been partly disarmed to act as an armed storeship; Captain Cochrane had specially asked for her, and Admiral Gambier agreed, with some reluctance. It has been alleged against Cochrane that he did not know about the great boom, thus showing a defect in his reconnaissance; but it is far more probable that he did know, and kept the knowledge to himself, in case Gambier, with his well-known caution, should call the whole action off. Otherwise, why did he ask for the MEDIATOR, when a much smaller and cheaper ship would have served just as well as a fireship? It was because only a frigate had weight enough to break the boom, and Captain Woolridge was a man after his own heart, to whom he could confide the secret.

The explosion vessels were most formidable. Their bottoms were strengthened with logs jammed together to form a solid floor; on this were placed a large number of casks, holding altogether 1,500 barrels of gunpowder, roped together and tamped down to increase the force of the explosion; on top were hundreds of mortar shells and thousands of hand grenades, with fuses, the idea being that the explosion would ignite the fuses as well as throwing the projectiles far and wide.

The operation began at 8.30 p.m. on the evening of 11th April 1809, with a strong wind from the north-west, and the tide with the fireships, the MEDIATOR leading. Lord Cochrane naturally took the leading explosion vessel, with Lieutenant Bissell and four volunteers. This is the most dangerous of all naval operations: to take a ship crammed with explosives into a fortified harbour against a powerful fleet fully prepared for the attack. A single hit on the terrible cargo, and not a fragment of the crew would be available for burial. Fireships were quite often used, particularly in the seventeenth century, but the explosion vessel was very rare indeed. (It has, however, been used twice in this century, when Lieutenant Sandford thrust his submarine under the mole at Zeebrugge, and in the second war when Captain Beattie rammed the CAMPBELL-TOWN into the dock-gates of St Nazaire. Never were Victoria Crosses better earned.)

In this case the explosion vessels were not very successful. One of them appears to have been swept away prematurely, and although her crew were on board either they did not light the fuse or the fuse failed. The other two both lighted their fuses, Captain Cochrane about ten minutes later than the other, and took to their boats in very rough sea conditions. Unfortunately, both vessels were stopped by the boom, which had not yet been broken by the MEDIATOR, and the effect of their terrific explosions was largely moral. Some of the fireships were ignited far too soon, and ran ashore before reaching the boom; but when Captain Woolridge broke the boom there were six other fireships, which, taking their time from the MEDIATOR, did not start their fires until they were past the boom, and the wind and tide were bound to bring the fireships right amongst the French fleet.

Few battles go precisely to plan; the boom had delayed the explosion vessels and the fireships, but now, as the blazing ships bore down on the French fleet, the rough weather made it impossible for the boats of the fleet to carry out their assigned task of boarding the fireships and towing them ashore. Moreover, who could tell that there were not more explosion vessels behind the sheet of flame which the gale blew in front of the advancing fireships? It would be an exaggeration to say that there was panic on board the French ships, but there was certainly a well-founded alarm. Every ship except one, the *Foudroyant*, which was in the rearmost of the lines, either cut or slipped her cables in order to get some steerage-way to avoid the desperate peril. Of those, one, the *Cassard*, anchored again about a quarter of a mile ahead of the *Foudroyant*; every one of the rest went on shore, and that at the top of the tide. Cochrane regained the IMPERIEUSE on the falling tide, stood out a little into deeper water, and re-anchored where he could observe the whole of the Aix road. He was tolerably content; his scheme had worked; all that was now necessary was for a few of the ships of the line to sail in and finish the job on the next tide.

This did not happen.

As soon as it was light enough Cochrane began making signals by semaphore to the CALEDONIA, as follows:

4.48 a.m. Half the fleet can destroy the enemy; seven on shore.

6.40 a.m. Eleven on shore.

7.40 a.m. Only two afloat.

9.30 a.m. Enemy preparing to heave off.

This last signal stirred even Lord Gambier into some kind of action, and at 9.35 a.m. he signalled the fleet to weigh, but delayed the execution of the order by calling a conference of all captains on board the CALEDONIA. This took more than an hour, after which the fleet got under way, but at 11.30 a.m. reanchored three miles north of the Île d'Aix, and six miles from the grounded French fleet. By this time the IMPERIEUSE had gone in to her former station abeam the south end of the island. Admiral Gambier now sent into the roads his only bomb-ketch, the ETNA, covered by three small gun-brigs, with orders to take position for bombarding the vessels aground. Captain Bligh of the VALIANT, 74, was ordered to take under his command the BELLONA and REVENGE, 74s, and also the frigates and smaller ships, and to anchor them where they could move in if necessary; this squadron anchored about half-way between the fleet and the IMPERIEUSE.

The French had not been idle during the low tide period. The two battleships still afloat had got up their topmasts, which had been taken down by general order. All those on shore had carried out, by boat, anchors which were laid well out, with the intention of kedging off at the top of the next tide. They put overboard most of their water, which they could replace, and many guns, which they might hope to retrieve. As the tide rose, the ships which had been badly heeled over began to rise unharmed, largely due to Vice-Admiral Allemand's foresight in having their upper masts struck down, for if they had heeled so far over with their top- and top-gallant-masts rigged they must either have cut them away or else filled before they could right themselves. At 12.45 p.m. the *Foudroyant* and *Cassard* made sail and steered for the Charente river, but grounded on the mud bar at the entrance. Three more of the stranded ships managed to kedge off, but also stuck on the mud-bar; and the great *Ocean* seemed to be moving.

Nothing could be more exasperating to a man like Cochrane than to witness the enemy escaping into safety, after all his exertions, simply because of the inertia of his admiral. By 1 p.m. all that had gone in were the bomb-ketch and three little brigs, and now Cochrane, without orders, weighed anchor; but to conceal the fact for a little he kept the ship's head still up, and drifted in with the tide stern first. The nearest French ships were the *Calcutta*, 50, a captured East India ship, and the *Aquilon* and *Varsovie*, 74s, all three on the rocky Palles shoal. Cochrane engaged the *Calcutta*, at the same time signalling for help. For very shame Gambier could not leave him unsupported, and at 2 p.m. ordered in the INDEFATIGABLE, and later the whole of the advanced squadron. All those ships concentrated on the three French ships which were hard and fast on the Palles, and made no serious attempt on those which were getting out of the mud and making for the safety of the river. The stranded vessels shortly surrendered; the *Calcutta* was set on fire by a midshipman sent to accept her surrender, and the other two were fired by Captain Bligh's orders, shortly after 3 a.m. on the morning of the 13th April; the *Tonnerre*, hopelessly on the rocks further south, was fired by her own men, before they took to their boats.

At 6.30 a.m. Captain Bligh led all the heavy ships out of the Aix roads, leaving Cochrane in command of the small craft. As the INDEFATIGABLE passed, Cochrane hailed Captain Rodd, to suggest that they should attack the *Ocean*, one on either quarter; Rodd prudently replied that he was under Captain Bligh's orders. Half an hour later came along the PALLAS, Cochrane's old command, with Captain George Seymour, the same who, in the KINGFISHER, had towed out the PALLAS after the action with the *Minerve*, and who, fifty years later, as Admiral Sir George Seymour, was to be a pall-bearer at his comrade's funeral in Westminster Abbey. He now hailed Cochrane, 'Shall I go or stay?' 'Stay by all means, if you have no orders to the contrary.' The PALLAS and all the small ships immediately anchored near the IMPERIEUSE, to wait until the tide served. By 11 a.m. the smaller ships came within range of the *Ocean, Regulus* and *Indienne*, still on the mud at the mouth of the river, the BEAGLE, 18-gun brig-sloop, Captain Woolcombe, taking the brunt, as she was armed with 32-pounder carronades. The two frigates were unable to get within decisive range, and after battering away for five or six hours the flotilla was forced to retire on the falling tide, at 4 p.m.

About noon, while the action was in progress, Cochrane received a letter from Lord Gambier, politely and praisefully phrased, but directing him to rejoin the flag-ship. Cochrane replied that he could destroy the ships on shore, which he hoped his lordship would approve. At 9 a.m. the admiral signalled to Cochrane to communicate with Captain Wolfe of the AIGLE, who was ordered to supersede Cochrane in the command inside the roads. At noon the AIGLE joined the IMPERIEUSE, and Captain Wolfe handed over the definite order, on which the IMPERIEUSE joined the CALEDONIA in the Basque roads; and next day, the 15th April, sailed for home, with Captain Sir Harry Neale, Captain of the Fleet, and Lord Gambier's despatches. Meanwhile the fleet lay in Basque roads for another fortnight watching the French getting their ships up the river without much interference from the British.

Lord Gambier's despatches did full justice to Lord Cochrane's exploits, and he was created a Knight of the Bath for his services. He was, however, obsessed with the idea that he had, from mere spite and jealousy, been prevented from achieving, with a few frigates, a victory comparable to that of the Nile. There can be no doubt of Gambier's courage after his handling of the DEFENCE on the glorious first of June; but he was a deep-sea sailor, and distrusted the shoals and tides inshore. His flag-ship, the CALEDONIA, was Britain's newest and best battleship; what if he had lost her by an error in the timing of the tide? And no doubt there were plenty of jealous officers to suggest that it was as well to send this firebrand captain home, on honourable terms, before he managed again to get the deep-water fleet involved among the shoals. But Cochrane took his recall as a personal affront and launched against Gambier a political assault, in which he found more dangerous and treacherous waters than he ever met on the Biscay shore. We may leave him here, for he never commanded a frigate again; the last word lies with Napoleon. 'Cochrane could not only have destroyed all the ships,' he said on St Helena, 'but he might and would have taken them out, had your admiral supported him as he ought to have done . . . The

French admiral was an *imbécile*, but yours was just as bad.
I assure you, if Cochrane had been supported, he would have
taken every one of the ships.'

Few historians have disagreed with the verdict of the greatest of all the great captains.

II

Prize Money

Spanish gold! There was little other gold in Europe from 1500 to 1850. Thereafter the discoveries in Australia, in California, later in Alaska, and lastly in South Africa have quite eclipsed Latin America as the source of gold, although three-quarters of the world's silver still comes from former Spanish possessions in America. A little gold was brought from the west coast of Africa, whence our guinea, but this was a drop in a bucket compared with the treasure which flowed across the Atlantic. It has been estimated that between 1500 and 1820 there were 17,000 voyages of treasure ships from America to Spain, carrying £4,000,000,000 sterling at sovereign value, five times as much in present paper. Naturally, everybody wanted to get in on an act like this, but the Spanish colonies were very firmly closed against all nations. Unabashed pirates such as Drake could get away with a lot, but the only legal method was to pick a quarrel with the Spanish government and declare war. By a curious coincidence, every time Britain has been reluctantly dragged into hostilities with Spain, there have been Spanish treasure ships at sea. Cromwell's war on Spain had no possible justification; his speech of 17th September 1656 to Parliament explaining it is the most confused and confusing of all his turgid orations, so different from his actions; but when, the next month, General-at-Sea Blake sent thirty-eight wagon-loads of gold and silver from Portsmouth to the Tower, the reason for the war was plain to all men, and they had a day of national thanksgiving. The War of Jenkin's Ear, begun in 1739, had no possible political justification, but one was provided by Commodore Anson when he took the Manila galleon, the *Nostra Signora de Cabadonga*, and brought the

CENTURION into Portsmouth on 15th June 1744 to send thirty-two wagons of treasure to the Tower. When, near the end of the Seven Years War, Britain declared war on Spain in January 1762 for no clearly discernible reason, it so happened that the Spanish treasure-frigate *Hermione* was at sea, and was swiftly picked up by two British frigates, which divided between them an all-time record in prize money.

This popular pastime was regulated by an Act of 1708, which laid down the proportions into which the value of the prize was to be divided. There were certain Droits of the Crown, but these were kept in reserve; in general, the full value of the prize, ship and cargo, went to the captors, as follows: the captain had three-eighths, of which he gave one to the flag officer under whom he served; the other officers, down to sergeant of Marines, had three-eighths, in three categories which ensured that the more senior had the bigger share; and the remaining two-eighths went to the rest of the crew, again shared according to seniority. Nor was this all: in the case of warships captured or destroyed, Admiralty paid head-money at the rate of £5 per head of the enemy crew at the commencement of the engagement. This was to encourage doubtful captains to engage warships rather than seek the easier and more lucrative merchant prizes; moreover, a successful engagement with a warship meant probable promotion, which never rewarded captors of merchantmen.

It is, fortunately, no part of our business to clarify the political reasons why Spain, ally of Britain in 1795, should become the ally of France and declare war on Britain on 2nd October 1796; but the timing was certainly injudicious, for Spanish treasure ships were at sea, and the frigates were at sea too, and within a fortnight made their pounce.

On the 15th of October, about 150 miles west of Vigo, the 38-gun frigate NAIAD, Captain William Pierrepont, at 8 p.m. discovered in the dusk two large sails and went in chase; by midnight they were ascertained to be Spanish, and frigates of some force, now steering to the south-east under all sail, the wind being dead aft. They were in fact the 34-gun frigates *Santa Brigida*, Captain Pillon, and *Thetis*, Captain de Mendoza, from Vera Cruz with treasure, and ordered for any port in Spain which they could make. A British 38-gun frigate had no reason to avoid combat with two Spanish 34s, especially if they were suspected of bearing treasure, and the NAIAD continued in pursuit under all possible sail. At 3.30 in the morning of the 16th another large sail was descried to the south-west, which came up and made herself known to be the ETHALION, 38 guns, Captain James Young. At dawn two more frigates appeared and joined in the chase, both 32-gun 12-pounders, the ALCMENE, Captain Henry Digby, and the TRITON, Captain John Gore. Of the four, Captain Pierrepont was the S.N.O.

The chase continued through the morning, the *Thetis* leading the *Santa Brigida*, and the ETHALION, the best sailer, leading the British line. At 7 a.m. the two Spanish ships separated, on which Captain Pierrepont ordered the ETHALION to pass the rear Spaniard and chase the *Thetis*, which was done, although Captain Young could not forbear giving the *Santa Brigida* a broadside in passing, at 9 a.m. By 11.30 a.m. the ETHALION came up with the *Thetis*; after a desultory running fight they came alongside, and after two full broadsides the *Thetis* hauled down her colours, having had one man killed and nine wounded, while the ETHALION had no casualties whatever.

The *Santa Brigida* was a very good sailer, and her captain evidently had a good knowledge of the dangerous coast he was now approaching. Making south, he rounded Cape Finisterre very close to the rocks, so close that the TRITON, first in pursuit, touched the rocks at seven knots, at 5 a.m. on the 17th. She got off, and by 7 a.m. was able to open fire on the *Santa Brigida*, which now threw overboard her anchors and boats, to aid her sailing; but the ALCMENE came up between her and the port of Muros, for which she was making. The *Santa Brigida* now tried to throw off her pursuers by elaborate manœuvres among the rocks of Commarurto in the entrance of Ria de Muros, but the NAIAD now came up and, surrounded by three powerful opponents, the *Santa Brigida* had no option but to surrender. Captain Don Antonio Pillon had shown the utmost courage and tenacity during a chase of thirty-two hours, and superb seamanship in attempts to gain port. His loss was 2 killed and 8 wounded, the British ships 1 killed and 10 wounded.

The result of the odds of at least four to two could readily be predicted; what made it interesting was the loot. Besides a cargo of valuable commodities such as cochineal and indigo, the two ships had between them about a thousand boxes each containing 3,000 silver dollars, besides odd bags and kegs and some gold. There can have been few literate persons in the squadron who were not doing pleasing little sums during the short voyage to Plymouth, where they arrived on the 21st November. The treasure was conveyed in sixty-three wagons to the citadel of Plymouth, and thence to London. The prize-money was divided thus:

Each Captain	£40,730
Each Lieutenant	5,091
Warrant-Officers	2,468
Midshipmen, etc.	791
Each Seaman and Marine	182

One has to consider that the rate of pay per annum did not exceed £150 for a frigate captain, £75 for a lieutenant, and £12 for an ordinary seaman. A captain would have to serve for 250 years to earn the money he picked up in a couple of easy days; and even the humblest seaman could set himself up in a cosy pub. It was very wise of Admiralty to allot these astounding prizes; it was like the football pools and the lotteries: I know that the chance is remote, but all the same, people have in fact won such prizes, and why should the next one not be me? Honour and glory are excellent things, but so are silver and gold; and if all are to be had in the same engagement, let us go heartily about it!

The next really big prize had some dubious aspects. Spain was at peace with Britain, but had entered into a special relationship with France, which included among other advantages an annual subsidy of about three million sterling, more than a third of the whole Spanish revenues. The British government received information that an armament was being prepared at Ferrol, and that French troops had crossed the border and were marching to Ferrol; an attack on Britain was projected, and waited only for the arrival of the next treasure fleet. The British government now resolved to cut off the subsidy at its source, and detain the treasure on the seas. This was really an act of war without war being declared, which in those gentlemanly days was considered highly immoral. However, the decision was taken, and orders were sent to

Cornwallis, off Brest, Sir Alexander Cochrane, off Ferrol, and Nelson, off Toulon, each to detach two good frigates to cruise off Cadiz and intercept the treasure fleet, and detain them until the pleasure of the British government should be known; but to refrain from any act of hostility unless the enemy, or friend, began a combat.

Four of the detailed frigates assembled off Cape Santa Maria, the southernmost point of Portugal, and commenced their patrol, the ships being INDEFATIGABLE, 44, Captain Graham Moore, MEDUSA, 32, 18-pounders, Captain Gore, AMPHION, 32, 18-pounders, Captain Sutton, and LIVELY, 38, Captain Hammond. On 5th October 1804, being about 30 miles southwest of the cape and 100 miles west of Cadiz, they sighted the expected squadron, which consisted of the 40-gun frigate *Medea*, with Rear-Admiral Don Joseph Bustamente, and the 34-gun frigates *Fama*, *Clara*, and *Mercedes*. On the approach of the British squadron, the Spaniards formed for battle in line ahead, *Fama*, *Medea*, *Mercedes*, *Clara*, on which the British adopted the same formation, MEDUSA, INDEFATIGABLE, AMPHION and LIVELY, thus giving the biggest ship to the INDEFATIGABLE, a very powerful frigate, as we have seen. The two squadrons continued for some time side by side, about thirty yards apart, when Captain Moore hailed the *Medea* to shorten sail; no reply was given, so a shot was fired across her bows, and she complied. Lieutenant Arscott was now sent on board her, to inform the rear-admiral what were the orders of the British squadron, and to urge him to comply without making necessary the use of force. The boat did not return for some time, and Captain Moore made a signal for her to return, and fired another shot ahead of the *Medea*. Lieutenant Arscott now returned with a negative reply, on which Moore fired another gun ahead of the *Medea*, and bore down on her weather bow. At once the *Mercedes* fired into the AMPHION, and the *Medea* fired into the INDEFATIGABLE; whereon that ship made the order for battle and a hot engagement commenced.

Within ten minutes the *Mercedes* blew up alongside the AMPHION, with a tremendous explosion which blew her to fragments with all in her, except about forty men who were rescued from the forecastle which broke off and floated for a time. A few minutes after, the *Fama* struck her colours, but when the MEDUSA ceased fire she rehoisted them and made off, with the MEDUSA in hot pursuit. About twenty minutes after the commencement, the *Medea*, which had been suffering from the 24-pounder broadsides of the INDEFATIGABLE, found the AMPHION coming up on her other bow, and struck her colours. Five minutes later the *Clara* also struck, thus releasing the LIVELY, a very fast ship, to go in pursuit of the *Fama*, which she overtook at the same time as the MEDUSA; now the *Fama* hauled down her colours and was taken in possession. The whole action was over by 1.15 p.m.

The British casualties were very small: 2 killed and 4 wounded in the LIVELY, 3 wounded in the AMPHION by fragments from the explosion of the *Mercedes*, none in the other ships. In the Spanish ships there were more: *Medea*, 2 killed and 10 wounded; *Fama*, 11 killed and 50 wounded; *Clara*, 7 killed and 20 wounded; and *Mercedes*, 240 killed. It is clear that the Spaniards fought with the greatest courage against a much more powerful squadron, especially after the loss of the *Mercedes*, and made every endeavour to carry out their orders and get into Cadiz. The *Fama* was criticised for making off after striking, but we are not fully aware of all the circumstances, and her casualty list shows that whatever the reason it was not cowardice.

There was one particularly unfortunate episode of this battle. A Captain Alvear of the Spanish Navy had spent thirty years in Montevideo, during which time he had acquired a modest fortune of £30,000, a wife, four daughters and five sons; and having decided to return to Spain, he embarked with his all on the *Mercedes*, for quick and safe transport. When the British squadron approached he and his eldest son transferred to the *Medea*, possibly at the request of the rear-admiral, as they were both fluent in English. From this ship he witnessed the explosion which at once annihilated his nine family and the fortune on which he had hoped to support them. Nothing could possibly make up for the loss of his family, except the coincidence whereby one son remained to him; but it is pleasing to record that, in an age when it was possible for politicians to be gentlemen, the British government restored to him the whole of his pecuniary loss.

The prize was very rich; having sailed from Montevideo, it carried the produce of the southern part of South America. There were sealskins, seal oil, vicuna wool, bars of tin and copper, and dollars and gold ingots to the amount of two millions sterling.* However, in stepped the Droits of the Crown aforementioned. Undoubtedly there had been an action fought and plenty of blood shed, under the orders of the government, which surely constituted warfare; but war had not been declared, and government chose to regard it as a police action in time of peace; hence the Droits of the Crown swallowed most of the loot. However, the squadron was given a quarter of a million as a sop, and as the captains would have about £15,000 apiece, they would be able to soak their sop in Madeira. Had the action taken place the following January, after the formal declaration of war between the two powers, this would have been the richest prize ever.

There are a number of other instances of prize-money scattered throughout this book. In general, the system went on the time-honoured principle of giving to him that hath. Almost every admiral commanding a station became a rich man, with the exception, perhaps, of Nelson, who received great emoluments but had rather an expensive way of life; when he died, he was paying £500 a year in interest on borrowed money. But at least half a dozen of his coevals made between two and three hundred pounds, worth a million in today's paper, and it was reckoned that a tour of duty as C-in-C of either the East or the West Indies was worth £100,000. These sums, too, represented only an eighth of what was collected by the other officers and men.

With so much money around loose, there were bound to be pickings. It was usual for officers to appoint agents to look after their prize interests, and many of those agents became very rich men. Within the prize system itself there was plenty of peculation, against which Lord Cochrane raged in vain. One safeguard was that as permanent paid officers of every prize court were two, one called proctor and one called marshal, who were supposed to be some sort of check on each other. When in June 1810 Lord Cochrane paid a visit to the prize court at Malta, to inquire about the money for the prizes he had taken years ago, he found that in that court the mar-

* A number of historiographers, following James, have put the amount at one million; I prefer Alison, who was a Member of Parliament, read Captain Moore's despatches, and took part in the debates on the matter.

shal and the proctor were one and the same person, named Jackson. One half of him held consultations with the other half, at a fee, and one half attested the other's signature, also at a fee. Cochrane expressed himself so freely about the corruption inside and outside the court that the two halves of Jackson agreed to have him arrested for insulting the court, and ordered the deputy marshal, named Chapman, to take him in custody. Cochrane refused arrest, on the grounds that Chapman was illegally appointed, being already deputy auctioneer! The appointed auctioneer lived in London and had no other activity than collecting his fees. Afraid to act, Chapman followed Cochrane about Malta for several days, but at length resigned his deputy marshal office, another was appointed more legally, and Cochrane was put in prison. Here he refused to supply himself with provisions, and the dual Jackson, who began to wish he had not been so high-handed, gave him an open order on the best hotel; Cochrane made full use of this, and entertained the Naval officers on the station to long, sumptuous and well-lubricated dinners in the prison. On 2nd March he was taken to court, which could not determine what to try him for and begged him to go on bail, which he refused. Eventually a comic-opera escape from the prison was arranged, and the gig of the EAGLE put him on board a packet-ship bound for England, where he arrived before the officials of double-duty Jackson had finished searching Malta for him. He made several motions in the House of Commons on those corruptions, all which motions were negatived without a division.

The fact is that at that period peculation and corruption were accepted as something regrettable, but just to be accepted, in the same way as we regard the fearful slaughter on the highways today. In both cases, it is felt that one can't do a thing about it, the reason being the same in both cases: the strength of the vested interests involved. Government grossly under-paid all its employees, and expected them to make it up to themselves, by fees legal or illegal, and in the case of the Navy, by prize-money. It was an intrinsic part of the Naval structure, very popular with the officers and men, and cost the government nothing. It was impossible to dispense with it, and if there were always dirty fingers in the dish, that was just one of those things which one finds everywhere.

12

Squadron Action

It is difficult to understand general European strategy at the beginning of the nineteenth century without fully realising what an important European power was the Ottoman Empire. It included almost the whole of modern Yugoslavia, half of Rumania, and the whole of Bulgaria and Greece. Belgrade and Bucharest were Moslem cities. Turkey in Europe was more extensive and populous than any western European state, and beyond lay a vast ramshackle empire including all Asia Minor, Arabia, Egypt, and indeterminate border regions. Not long before, historically speaking, under strong leadership the Turks had been thundering at the gates of Vienna, and had been turned back from the complete domination of the Mediterranean at Lepanto. True, generations of weak rule had weakened the Ottoman Empire; but if a resolute organiser were to make his way to its throne, it would once again be one of the great powers.

By the provisions of the Peace of Tilsit, Napoleon took the province of Illyria, which stretches from Trieste for more than three hundred miles down the coast of the Adriatic Sea. Instead of handing it over to some satellite ruler, Napoleon incorporated the province as an integral part of metropolitan France, under his direct rule. He now had a French province which had two hundred miles of frontier with the Ottoman Empire. With his mind always a tiger-spring ahead, he could visualise building up a great army in Illyria; given security in the rest of Europe, in one campaign Constantinople would be his. Meanwhile, he had to keep the Adriatic open for his supply ships, and for this purpose a large number of frigates were stationed there, mostly based on Ancona, while the shipyards of Venice were urged into production, especially of 74-gun ships.

The British frigates were based chiefly on Malta and Sicily, but managed a forward base in the Adriatic by capturing the island of Lissa (now Vis). This is a small island, about ten miles by five miles, with an excellent harbour in Port St George, and several other good anchorages. Batteries were erected and provided with plenty of guns and stores, but the garrison was never sufficient for a point of such importance, which has always been held to be the key to the Adriatic. With this base for refuge in need, the small British vessels had a wonderful time in the Adriatic, capturing cargo ships at sea or cutting them out in harbour. It was not possible to blockade all the fine harbours, but they captured a large percentage of all the shipping that stirred.

The French could not leave such a thorn alone, and made repeated attempts to recapture the island. In October 1810, in the absence of any British warship, a squadron under Commodore Dubourdieu actually landed a considerable body of troops, and had possession of the island for several hours, but withdrew on hearing news of the approach of a British squadron. The following spring a more determined attack was ordered; Commodore Dubourdieu now had four 40-gun frigates, the *Favorite* (flag), *Corona*, *Danae* and *Flore*, two 32-gun frigates, the *Bellona* and *Carolina*, a 16-gun brig *Mercure*, a 10-gun schooner, the 6-gun xebec, and two gun-boats; also a battalion of infantry under Colonel Gifflenga, to form the garrison of the island after capture; a force of about 300 guns and 2,500 men, all told. This powerful squadron sailed from Ancona towards evening on 11th March 1811, and hove-to off the north shore of Lissa shortly after midnight the following day. There they were reported at 3 a.m on the 13th March to the defending British squadron. This consisted of the 32-gun frigate (18-pounders) AMPHION, Captain William Hoste (S.N.O.), 38-gun frigate ACTIVE, Captain James Gordon, 32-gun frigate CERBERUS, Captain Henry Whitby, and the 22-gun ship VOLAGE, Captain Phipps Hornby; a total force of about 150 guns and 900 men, rather worse odds than one to two.

Admiralty could not spare many 74s for the Adriatic operations, and few large frigates; to make up for this, they sent some of their very best officers with good crews, to make up for too few and too light ships. Captain William Hoste, in command of the squadron, had the inestimable advantage of having been reared on the quarter-deck under Nelson himself, who took an interest in the promising youth and helped forward his promotion. Since coming to the Adriatic, both he and the other frigate captains (who were not always under his command, being detached from time to time) had been very active in their inshore duties, capturing many prizes, and also engaged in the less remunerative work of correcting charts, a tedious but, in this case at least, a rewarding occupation.

At dawn the French squadron could be plainly descried, about two miles to windward, the wind fair at NNW. Their strength could also be clearly understood; but under Nelson's midshipman there could be no question of 'fight or flee?' He formed his squadron in close line ahead, himself leading in the AMPHION, followed by the ACTIVE as the most powerful ship, the VOLAGE as the weakest, while the CERBERUS brought up the rear. Meanwhile the French formed in two divisions, each line consisting of three frigates and some smaller ships, so that each division was more powerful than the whole British squadron. Having the weather-gauge, they bore down on the compact squadron, in the hope, no doubt, of breaking the line. Hoste now made a signal 'remember Nelson!' and the loud cheers with which this was greeted in all the ships told the captain that all his men were with him.

Commodore Dubourdieu in the *Favorite* was leading the windward division, and decided that the close and steady formation of the British line would be hard to break; he therefore stood ahead, meaning to cross the bows of the AMPHION with his division, and thus get the British squadron within the cross-fire of both of his divisions. The heavy fire of the two leading ships made this a difficult manœuvre, and he decided to board the AMPHION, when his great superiority of numbers must tell. Accordingly he assembled a large boarding-party on the forecastle, and approached the quarter-deck of the AMPHION; but that ship had on her quarter-deck a $5\frac{1}{2}$-inch howitzer, loaded with 750 musket-balls, which was discharged

LESSINA (French)

20 MILES

WIND N.N.W. FAIR

LISSA

9 SAN FIORENZE taking possession of *Piémontaise*

10 ALCESTE and ACTIVE capturing the *Pomone*

11 *Constitution* escaping from a British squadron

12 GUERRIERE captured by *Constitution*

13 MACEDONIAN captured by *United States*

14 JAVA captured by *Constitution*

15 *Chesapeake* boarded and captured by SHANNON

16 *Essex* (left) engaged and captured by PHOEBE and CHERUB

with accuracy at a range of about ten yards. The destruction was fearful; there fell the commodore, the captain, and most of the senior officers, so that the command devolved upon Colonel Gifflenga, with a junior sea officer to work the ship. The *Favorite* gave up the attempt to board, and kept on working forward of the AMPHION, which was just what Hoste wanted, for he had corrected his charts. At the right moment —the last possible moment—he signalled for all his ships to wear about simultaneously, and when the *Favorite*, ahead, also wore, she ran upon the rocks in a hopeless condition, so near had Hoste led her to the shore. About 200 of her men escaped to shore, armed, having set fire to the ship, which blew up with a great explosion about 4 p.m.

While wearing, the CERBERUS had her rudder damaged by a shot, and could not get round so handily as the VOLAGE, which now became the leading ship and the AMPHION the rear. The *Flore*, the second ship in the weather division, now was able to carry out the manœuvre which the Commodore had tried so disastrously; she crossed the stern of the AMPHION and came up on her leeward side, while the *Bellona* approached on the other, so that the AMPHION was caught between the fires of two ships, one of them equal to and the other larger than herself. In such a position, any captain would have been justified in surrendering; but Captain Hoste was not any captain: he had walked Nelson's quarter-deck. He could trust his seamen to work the ship through any manœuvre, however complicated, amid the storm of round-shot and musket-balls that came from almost every direction. With superb seamanship, the AMPHION made more sail, moved ahead, suddenly turned right across the bows of the *Flore*, wore again, into a position where

Battle of Lissa: The Approach

British ships in line ahead: AMPHION (flag) 32 guns, A; ACTIVE, 38 guns, B; VOLAGE, sloop, 22 guns, C; CERBERUS, 32 guns, D

French ships in two divisions: Windward division, *Favorite* (flag) 40 guns, 1; *Flore*, 40 guns, 2; *Bellona*, 32 guns, 3; *Mercure*, brig, 16 guns, 7; 6-gun xebec, 8; 10-gun schooner, 9
Leeward division, *Danae*, 40 guns, 4; *Corona*, 40 guns, 5; *Carolina*, 32 guns, 6; 2 gunboats, 10 and 11

LESSINA (French)

20 MILES

WIND N.N.W. FAIR.

LISSA

her whole larboard broadside could bear on the starboard bow of the *Flore*, while that ship completely screened her from the fire of the *Bellona*. From this favourable position the AMPHION opened such a fire that in a few minutes the *Flore* struck her colours. Meanwhile the *Bellona* had passed the stern of the *Flore*, and now re-engaged the AMPHION; but again by superior seamanship the AMPHION was enabled to get a position on the *Bellona*'s bow from which she could rake the ship with very little reply, and after a few broadsides the *Bellona* too struck her colours.

The AMPHION now made a signal for a general chase, and sent a party to take possession of her prizes; the *Bellona* was duly taken over; but seeing the shortage of boats in the AMPHION, the *Flore* now made sail and escaped, much to the chagrin of all on board the victor, which was too much cut about in the rigging to give chase.

While all this was going on, the head of the line was being attacked by the three frigates of the lee division. The 40-gun *Danae* came close alongside the little VOLAGE, which, however, was armed with 32-pounder carronades, at that range quite as effective as the long 18s of the frigate, which made haste to lengthen the range. Meanwhile the CERBERUS was closely engaged by the *Corona* and, at a much greater distance, the *Carolina*. Both the VOLAGE and the CERBERUS were in serious trouble, when up came the ACTIVE, which the French frigates had tended to avoid; on her approach the three French frigates made off to the eastward under all sail, chased by the ACTIVE, which came up with the *Corona*, the largest of the three, about 12.30 p.m., and fought her for two hours, when she too surrendered. The *Carolina* and *Danae* escaped to the

Battle of Lissa: The critical Manœuvre

Hoste orders his ships to wear right about simultaneously. The *Favorite*, which has been trying to head him, runs ashore and is wrecked. The *Flore* and the *Bellona* wear to attack the AMPHION. The *Danae* and the *Corona* wear to attack the new leading ships, while the *Carolina* shows no great eagerness to engage. The CERBERUS, having a shot in her rudder, does not get about very handily, and drops astern of the little VOLAGE, which becomes the leading ship of the squadron.

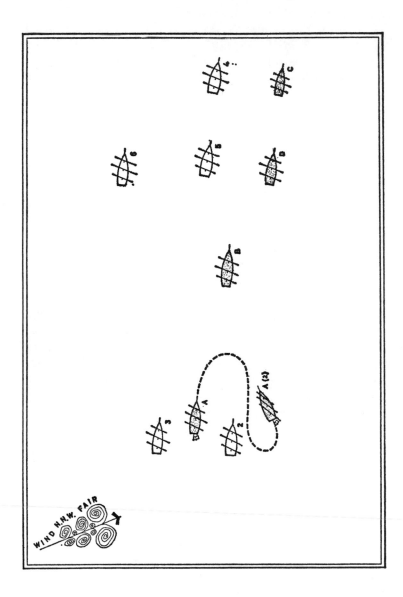

WIND N.N.W. FAIR

protection of the batteries of Lesina, where they were joined by the *Flore*, which had surrendered and then escaped (not at all the done thing). The small craft scattered and all got into some port or other.

The British ships were all more or less knocked about in rigging and hull, but nothing that fishing, splicing and patching could not make good temporarily. The losses were heavy, a total of 45 killed and 145 wounded among the four ships; yet less than might have been expected in so desperate an attack. The French losses are not precisely ascertained, but have been estimated at about 700, with some probability, apart from prisoners. The 200 men who got ashore from the *Favorite* marched boldly to Port St George, where they hoped to seize shipping enough to carry them to Lesina, only twenty miles away; but they were prevented by two young midshipmen, James Lew and Robert Kingston, who had been left there in charge of some prizes, and who now assumed command of all the ships in the port, under threat of what Captain Hoste would do when he returned. What he did do was to send a flag of truce to Lesina to demand that the *Flore* be given up, as she had surrendered. The reply was as might be expected, and indeed no French captain's life would be worth a rap if he gave up a valuable ship on a point of honour; Napoleon had much more use for the ship.

Of the two prizes which were brought away, the *Corona*, which had been built the year before at Venice, was taken into the Royal Navy under the name of DAEDALUS, while the *Bellona* was bought in for a troopship (for which there was great demand) under the name of DOVER. This was a neat bit of prize-money, and in addition the four captains had a gold medal apiece, and all four first lieutenants were made commanders. At a later date Captain Hoste was knighted. Indeed,

Battle of Lissa: The Crisis of the Battle

AMPHION is engaged by both *Flore* and *Bellona*, one on each side; but by a masterly move Hoste disengages himself and takes a position on the starboard bow of the *Flore*, which now covers him from the *Bellona*; the *Flore* shortly surrenders. The CERBERUS and the VOLAGE are heavily engaged at great odds with the *Corona* and the *Danae*, with the *Caroline* in the offing. The ACTIVE is pushing up under all sail to assist.

WIND N.N.W. FAIR

6
4
2(2)
5
B
C
D
A
2
3

LESSINA (French)
4 MILES

they were worthy of every honour the country could bestow. Seldom in naval history has a squadron attacked another of more than twice its force, and so completely defeated it. It was only done by courage, skill and seamanship, and was a proof, if any were needed, of how well Hoste and his brother captains had trained their men and gained their complete confidence.

Note: In this chapter all the enemy ships are referred to as French; in fact the *Bellona, Carolina* and *Corona,* and some small ships, were Venetian, and fought under that flag, in a manner which would have done it credit in the greatest days of the Republic. In particular, Captain Pasqualigo of the *Corona* elicited the warm admiration of his opponents; he 'ennobled an already noble name'.

'I came home in the squadron with the prizes in 1811, and recollect to have heard Sir William Hoste, and the other officers engaged in that glorious conflict, speak in the highest terms of Pasqualigo's behaviour.'—*Lord Byron, in a note in an appendix to* 'The Doge of Venice'.

Battle of Lissa: The End of the Battle

Flore (2) has surrendered, but improperly sets sail again and makes off (2 (2)). *Bellona* has come around the stern of the *Flore,* but by another feat of seamanship Hoste engages her in an advantageous position and she surrenders. The ACTIVE is heavily engaged with the *Corona,* which will shortly surrender after a very honourable resistance. The other frigates are making off for Lessina; the small ships have scattered to make what port they can. The VOLAGE and the CERBERUS are licking their wounds.

13

The Big Frigates

Lord Palmerston once said, 'Only three people have ever really understood the Schleswig-Holstein business: the Prince Consort, who is dead; a German Professor, who has gone mad; and I, who have forgotten all about it.' Much the same might be said about the reasons why the United States of America declared war upon Great Britain on 18th June 1812. There had been grumblings for at least four years, but nothing which could not have been settled by negotiation; in fact, *was*, and twice, settled by negotiation; but on one occasion the British and on the other the American government refused to ratify what their envoys had agreed. The ostensible reason was the British blockade of Europe, proclaimed by Orders in Council; but these had been rescinded *before* hostilities actually commenced. Historians and commentators have advanced their simplifications of the complex motivations of an emerging nation, with which fortunately we have nothing to do—

> *'But one thing I'm sure*
> *That at Sheriffmuir*
> *A battle there was that I saw, man!'*

Apart from the *why*, the *when* of the American declaration of war is hard to understand. True, the news they had from Europe was of Napoleon's conference at Dresden, with almost all the sovereigns in western Europe tributary to his imperial power, while he reviewed an army of five hundred thousand men, superbly equipped. This may have seemed a good wagon to jump on, and they could not have known that within three days of the declaration of war, Wellington was to cross the Aguedo on the way to Salamanca, Vittoria and Toulouse; and within nine days Napoleon was to cross the Niemen, on the way to Moscow, Leipzig and Elba. But what they certainly did know was that the whole Navy of the United States consisted of 8 frigates and 12 sloops, of which 20, only 17 were available for sea service; and they also knew that Britain had 584 ships at sea in full commission, of which 102 were line-of-battle ships and 124 were frigates, with an immediate reserve of 18 battleships and 15 frigates. Moreover, the area of responsibility had diminished, since there were now no French or allied bases in all the seas of the world. The fleet with which Rear-Admiral Stopford had recently taken Java, with four line-of-battle ships and fourteen frigates, was at least three times stronger than the whole American Navy; nothing was easier than to call them home, and desire them to eat up the American Navy as they came by; but of course this did not happen.

The Royal Navy was suffering from a severe attack of superiority complex, resulting, not unnaturally, from almost twenty-two years of almost complete victories. The Navy of the United States consisted of only a few frigates: good enough, we have plenty of frigates on the West Indies and Halifax stations, let them deal with the situation. This was exactly the spirit with which, in 1914, Admiralty, with Winston Churchill as First Lord of the Admiralty and Jacky Fisher as First Sea Lord, sent out Rear-Admiral Craddock to Coronel with a mixed rag-bag of ships, manned mostly by reservists, to meet the crack cruiser squadron of the German Navy. It was the qualitative factor which they overlooked, and it was very difficult to tell them anything. In 1910–14, any Briton who dared to hint that the ships of the German Navy were better constructed, and their gunnery practice of a better standard, than the Royal Navy, was instantly branded as a traitor. In the same way, when Doctor Gregory, a well-known citizen of Edinburgh, said in 1808, 'The Americans are building long 46-gun frigates, which really carry 56 or 60 guns; when our 44s come to meet them, you will hear something new some of these days', of course nobody paid the least attention; what could a physician know about naval matters?

In fact the big American frigates were superior to any other frigate afloat, in two essentials; the ships themselves, and their crews.

The United States had in the great forests an endless supply of the finest ship-building timbers in the world. Northern white oak is only very slightly inferior to the Adriatic oak, while the pine and spruce for masts and spars was at least equal to the best the Baltic could produce. There was plenty of it, no need to scrimp, and only the selected best went into an American warship. To further ensure this, every American ship had an experienced captain standing by her during the whole course of her construction, a thing previously unknown, although now of course standard practice in all navies. Thus all American warships of whatever size were built of the very best materials, by skilled shipwrights, under strict and expert supervision. Class for class, they had no superior.

But the Americans were not content with class for class; they had to have something altogether superior to anything of the same nominal classification.

In 1794 it was decided to construct two 74-gun line-of-battle ships, and these were laid down; but due to changes in the political situation it was decided to finish them as frigates, but retaining, except for the extra gun-deck, the construction and sail-power of the 74. These were launched in 1797, as the *United States* and the *Constitution*, and rated as 44-gun frigates; in 1798 two more 44-gun frigates were built as frigates from the beginning, and therefore of slightly lighter construction and better sailing capacity, but still far bigger and more powerful than any other frigate in the world: the *President*, built at New York, and the *Philadelphia*, built at that city. All four 44-gun frigates actually mounted a main battery of thirty long 24-pounders, eighteen carronades, 42-pounders, on the quarter-deck, and on the forecastle six similar carronades and two long 24-pounders, a total of 56 guns, with a broadside of 768 pounds. By American measure they were all about 1,444 tons, but by British measure they were 1,533 tons. With their great length* and sail-power, they were the fastest warships in the world.

Not only were the big frigates larger and more powerful

* It is generally understood that the speed of a sailing vessel is limited by its water-line length, maximum speed under similar conditions varying as the square root of the L.W.L. Thus if a ship of 100 feet long does 10 knots, one of 144 feet should do 12 knots. There are of course some thousands of other considerations in the design of sailing ships.

than anything they need meet, they were far better manned. While Britain was raking the gaols to make up the 'quota', the Americans were rejecting all but skilled seamen of first-class physique. The reason, of course, was the small number of ships compared to the seamen available. The north-east states of the Union produced a race of bold and hardy seamen, manning a very large merchant marine, many of whom were unemployed as the British blockade tightened. The western states produced the most highly skilled riflemen in the world, and these constituted the Marines. Lastly, the ranks were supplemented by a large number of trained seamen, deserters from the Royal Navy. There were something like 5,000 deserters every year, of which about half were Able Seamen. During the Peace of Amiens, about 70,000 men were dismissed, or liable to be dismissed, from the Royal Navy, and many took service with the United States Navy, which was at that time engaged in naval operations against the Barbary States. It is highly probable that every large American frigate had a hundred British seamen aboard. When war was declared, some of these asked to be released from their service, but many did not. In action, these could be relied upon to the death, for it was death for them anyhow if they were captured.

One of the four big frigates was lost in the Mediterranean in 1804. The *Philadelphia*, Captain Bainbridge, had chased a ship which escaped into the harbour of Tripoli; but, in beating out, the *Philadelphia* ran on a rock, not marked on her charts. All efforts were made to float her off, anchors cut away, guns thrown overboard, without effect; and on the approach of some Tripolitan gun-boats the *Philadelphia* surrendered without resistance. In about two days the captors managed to float her, and took her into Tripoli harbour. Lieutenant Stephen Decatur, now first heard of, proposed to Commodore Preble to go into the harbour and burn her, which the Commodore at first thought too risky, but at length approved. On the 18th February Lieutenant Decatur, with seventy volunteers in a captured ketch, entered the harbour, boarded the *Philadelphia*, and after a sharp engagement captured her. She was immediately set on fire, and the boarding party made good their escape, having only four wounded.

There are some odd aspects of this story; if the *Philadelphia* could be captured by 70 small-arms men, how could she not have been defended by 300? And, having captured her, why was no attempt made to bring her out? A good deal may be put down to inexperience, but it would superficially appear that more might have been done to preserve what, after all, was more than an eighth of the whole American Navy of that date.

In those days of slow communication, it was very difficult for ships at sea to be informed of a declaration of war; the side which was going to declare war could give advance information to commanding officers, but the ships on the receiving end had to depend on unofficial rumours and otherwise wait until actually attacked. Thus when war was declared on the 18th of June 1812, a strong squadron was able to sail from New York on the 21st, the object being the Jamaica convoy, which had not the least idea of hostilities, and was making a leisurely course for Britain; a hundred richly laden merchantmen under the protection of a frigate and a brig; easy meat for the American squadron, which consisted of two of the big frigates, a 36-gun frigate and two brigs. However, when they were still some hundreds of miles west of the convoy, they came upon a solitary British frigate, and the whole squadron altered course to pursue her, the leading ship being the big frigate *President*, Commodore Rodgers.

The British frigate was the BELVIDERA, 36 guns, 18-pounders, Captain Richard Byron. He must have had some grave suspicions, for when the whole squadron approached him, quite unnecessarily if only for greeting and information, he stood away to the NE by E, about as close as he could haul to the wind which was at NW. Finding the squadron gaining on him, Captain Byron cleared for action, and shifted two long 18-pounders so as to fire through the sternports in his cabin, as well as bringing two 32-pounder carronades to the stern of the quarter-deck. All guns were loaded, but not primed, so that there should be no accidental shot on his part. The wind veered to WSW and decreased, so that by 4.20 the *President* was able to open fire with her bow-guns, three hits causing damage and casualties. The BELVIDERA returned fire with her well-prepared stern-chasers, the Captain and the First Lieutenant Sykes personally pointing the quarter-deck carronades, while Lieutenants Bruce and Campbell did the same for the

18-pounders in the cabin. Within a few minutes one of the *President*'s forward 24-pounders burst, a most serious accident, killing and wounding sixteen men, including the commodore, who had gone forward. The damage to the decks and side was severe, and put her chase-guns out of action for a considerable time.

Thus deprived of her forecastle armament, the *President* began yawing from side to side to allow her main battery guns to bear; and as this would allow the BELVIDERA to make away, the fire was directed mainly at the rigging, which was considerably damaged; however, as only the four stern-chasers could fire, the crew were set to replacing and splicing the rigging and fishing damaged spars. It requires no common steadiness and discipline to go aloft about this work with the shot of heavy broadsides screaming past the ears. The *President*, however, was gaining, and Captain Byron now ordered four anchors to be cut away, on which the BELVIDERA began to get ahead. The 36-gun frigate *Congress*, Captain Smith, now took up the chase about 6.30 p.m., and appeared to be gaining, although her shot was falling short. Captain Byron now threw overboard four of his boats and fourteen tons of water, and by 8 p.m. was two miles ahead of any pursuer; now the business was to fish the damaged main topmast, a difficult and risky job with the spar in position and the ship under way. However, it was done, and at 11 p.m. Captain Byron, now three miles ahead, altered his course to ESE, boomed out studding sails, and went ahead at such a rate that by midnight the American squadron gave up the chase.

This was a very neat little engagement, and reflects the greatest credit on Captain Byron and the ship's company of the BELVIDERA; but as they had been engaged in running away, they received no acknowledgement whatever from their government. Nevertheless, they had scored a notable victory, the saving of the Jamaica convoy. By keeping the whole American squadron hotly engaged from dawn to midnight of a long summer's day, in the wrong direction, and inflicting such injuries on the *President* that took another day to repair, they had ensured the convoy's escape. 'Lose not an hour', said Napoleon; and the big frigates had lost forty-eight.

On the 19th of August 1812 the *Constitution*, Captain Isaac Hull, about 500 miles south of Newfoundland, came up with the GUERRIERE, Captain Dacres, on her way to Halifax for a much-needed refit. This was a 38-gun 18-pounder frigate, a powerful vessel, but under-manned and in poor condition; she had been struck by lightning, which had damaged her mainmast and bowsprit, and her hull was leaky. She was no match for the big frigate, being 1,092 tons to 1,533, a much lighter broadside, and only 244 men against 460. However, when Captain Dacres descried the enemy frigate he shortened sail to allow her to come up, and at 5 p.m. opened fire, all her shot falling short.

Ten minutes later the *Constitution* opened up with a broadside so effective that the GUERRIERE began dodging about, in the hope of upsetting the aim of the American gunners; but in fact it had a far worse effect on the British. After half an hour of fairly long-range firing, Captain Hull decided to bring on a decisive action, and closed in. At about 6 p.m. the mizzen-mast of the GUERRIERE was shot away; it fell right aft, knocking a large hole in the ship's counter in which some of the rigging stuck, difficult to cut away, while the mast kept dragging astern like a sea-anchor. The *Constitution*, handled with great skill, now ranged athwart the bows of her opponent, raking her with tremendous broadsides to which she could only reply with a few bow-guns. Shortly the two ships fell foul, the bowsprit of the GUERRIERE tangling in the starboard mizzen-rigging of the *Constitution*. Captain Hull now decided on boarding, and his men assembled on the quarter-deck, while Captain Dacres went forward to the forecastle with his determined force to repel them. The Marines on both sides kept up a sharp and deadly fire at very close range. The officers were naturally the most conspicuous targets. The leaders of the two American boarding parties, the first lieutenant and the lieutenant of Marines, were both shot down, which caused some delay in preparation; and the sailing master was wounded. On the GUERRIERE, Captain Dacres was severely wounded in the back, but refused to leave the deck, while the sailing master and a master's mate were also wounded.

Now the GUERRIERE got her bowsprit free, and was able to get a good position across the stern of the *Constitution*, firing a broadside at so short a range that the burning wads set fire to the captain's cabin. But now the foremast came down, taking the mainmast with it, so that the GUERRIERE lay quite dismasted, while the *Constitution* ranged ahead to make some repairs to the rigging. Without masts to steady her, the GUERRIERE was rolling enough to dip her main deck guns in the sea, and there was grave danger of their breaking loose. Captain Dacres set a division to secure the guns, another to clear the decks of wreckage, and another to set a sail on the sprit-sail yard, which warships still carried but seldom used. However, as soon as the wind filled this little sail, the yard carried away. The *Constitution* now came up, and the GUERRIERE hauled down her colours from the stump of the mizzen-mast.

The casualties in the GUERRIERE were terribly severe, 78 killed and wounded, as against 14 in the *Constitution*. The ship was a shattered wreck, so much so that next morning the prize master hailed that she was sinking. The prisoners and prize crew were taken on board the *Constitution*, the wreck of the *Guerriere* was fired, and shortly blew up. Captain Hull repaired the slight damages to the *Constitution*, and on 30th August arrived at Boston to a hero's welcome, the thanks of the government, and a present of $50,000.

The *United States* was one of the big frigates which had been laid down as a 74-gun ship, and her construction was even more massive than usual for that heavy class; she sailed a little slower than the others, and was nicknamed 'The Wagon', hence, doubtless, the term 'battle wagon' for a more modern battleship. Provisioned for a long voyage, with an ample crew of picked seamen, and commanded by the fine officer Commodore Stephen Decatur, she was cruising in the Atlantic with no doubt the hope of intercepting some of the convoys from India. When about five hundred miles south of the Azores, at dawn on 12th October 1812, a sail was descried about twelve miles to windward, headed on a parallel track, both ships being as close-hauled as possible on a fresh wind from the SSE. This was a fine new 38-gun frigate, the MACEDONIAN, Captain John Surman Carden, rather under-manned as usual, with only 262 men and the extraordinary proportion of 35 boys; but a crew in good heart with excellent officers.

Immediately on sighting, the MACEDONIAN boomed out studding sails and bore away in pursuit. At first Commodore Decatur took her for a 74, no doubt deceived by the vast spread of canvas, and therefore wore away also, to get the wind more on the quarter, as he had, very properly, no intention of engaging a line-of-battle ship so far from any possibility of support. As the MACEDONIAN came closer, her single deck of guns became visible, and the *United States* put about and advanced to meet her, at the same time hoisting her colours, the broad pendant showing her to be commanded by a commodore and therefore one of the new '44s'. This caused no hesitation on the MACEDONIAN, for they had had no news for some time, had not heard of the GUERRIERE, did not know the power of these new big frigates, but were quite sure that a British 38-gun ship could capture any size of frigate afloat.

Being asked his opinion, Lieutenant Hope thought it would be best to continue the present course, which would bring her very close across the bows of the enemy, in the hopes of raking her; a good manœuvre, but dangerous if the enemy were clever enough. Captain Carden preferred to keep the advantage of the weather-gauge, which he already had, and hauled closer to the wind. As the two ships passed in opposite directions, the *United States* fired a broadside, without any effect, the range being too great for accuracy. Having got himself into the position he wanted, Captain Carden now put about and followed the *United States*, coming up on her windward quarter about 9.20 a.m., when the cannonade commenced. The first exchange brought down a small spar of the *United States*, but took the mizzen top-mast of the MACEDONIAN, letting her driver-gaff fall; so that the *United States* had now the advantage in sailing, and continued with the MACEDONIAN on her quarter, at a fairly long range, where the 24-pounders of the American were much more effective than the 18s of the British. Particular aim was taken at the carronades on the forecastle and quarter-deck, which were all dismounted and the bulwark shattered on the engaged side, before Commodore Decatur closed the range to a decisive distance.

Shortly after 11 a.m. the MACEDONIAN was a wreck; mizzen-mast gone, main and fore top-masts gone; nevertheless they set the only remaining sail on the foremast, to make enough way to come against the *United States* and try boarding her; however at that moment the fore-brace was shot away, and the sail swung round. The *United States* now passed the bows of the MACEDONIAN, without firing a shot, and stood away. The crew of the MACEDONIAN began cheering this surprising deliverance, but in fact the *United States* went off a little way to refill cartridges, having fired seventy broadsides in the action, using up all her ready cartridges. By noon, having filled a sufficiency and repaired some rigging, she tacked around and took up a position athwart the stern of the helpless MACEDONIAN; and the colours had to come down.

In this stout defence, the casualties of the MACEDONIAN were very heavy, amounting to 104 killed and wounded, as against 12 killed and wounded in the *United States*, which was also very little damaged, whereas the MACEDONIAN had more than 100 shot in her hull. Indeed, the two ships had to lie together for a fortnight until the *Macedonian* could be made fit to sail, and it was the 4th of December before they sighted Long Island. It is quite remarkable that during this long period, two weeks lying-to and five weeks passage, the two ships were never sighted by any British vessel. The *Macedonian* was purchased into the US Navy, with prize-money of $200,000 to the crew; along with the thanks of both Houses, a gold medal to the commodore and silver ones to the officers. These were well deserved; with hindsight, it is clear that the action could have no other ending, but this was by no means so clear before. Some bloodthirsty historians have criticised Decatur for not closing immediately, but in that case the 32-pounder carronades of the British ship would have been very effective; he was quite right to put them out of action before he closed. He won a complete victory with minimum loss, which should be the aim of every commander. There was every possibility that some British warship might come up, while there was no possibility whatever of American support. Had he fought a close action immediately and incurred severe damage, he would have been in a very poor position. His action at Tripoli had sufficiently shown the dashing lieutenant; this one showed the clear-headed and cautious commodore.

The government of the United States now decided to put a strong squadron into the Pacific, commanded by Commodore William Bainbridge, in the *Constitution*, along with the *Essex*, frigate, and the 18-gun *Hornet*. They were to sail from different ports and meet at Salvador (Bahia) in Brazil, not a good arrangement. The *Essex* sailed from the Delaware River on 27th October 1812, and the other two from Boston on the 30th, arriving off Salvador towards the end of December, where they found no sign of the *Essex*. The commodore ordered the *Hornet* into the port to make inquiries, while he took the *Constitution* about thirty miles off the coast.

The *Renommée* had been captured in an action off Madagascar by the ASTREA, Captain Schomberg, in February 1811, taken into the Royal Navy at Portsmouth and renamed JAVA, the former ship of that name having been lost (p. 80). On 17th August 1812 Captain Lambert, a brave and efficient officer, was commissioned to her, with orders to fit her out in order to convey to Bombay the new Governor, Lieutenant-General Hislop, with his suite, and also stores, largely copper, for ships which were building at Bombay. With the resources of Portsmouth the ship was quickly got ready; but to get a crew was a very different matter. With 140,000 seamen and Marines at sea, the barrel had been scraped clean. Officers and senior petty officers were easy, and 50 Marines were provided, 18 of them raw recruits, but good material. The 23 boys were easily found. 60 Irish landmen were put on board, along with 50 seamen suspected of mutinous intentions, from a sloop at Spithead. At length 292 out of 300 were got together. Captain Lambert naturally remonstrated about the poor quality and inexperience of his crew, but was laughingly assured that a voyage to Bombay and back, under his captaincy, would make sailors of them all; and besides, the chance of meeting an enemy was now very remote. At length, he was allowed to take eight real seamen, volunteers, from the RODNEY. He now had his complement, of whom, excluding the officers, less than fifty had ever been in action. Eventually he sailed on the 12th of November, having 397 people on board, including the Governor, his suite and servants; and having two East India merchantmen under his convoy.

As is well known, long before this period the study of winds and currents had shown that the best route to India was to make Madeira, then keep west of the Canaries and Cape Verde Islands and then S by SW almost to the coast of Brazil, then S by SE until latitude 35° South, and there pick up the great westerly wind which circles the world in 35° to 55° South; returning, the route is fairly near the African coast all the way, although it was usual, after touching at St Helena and sighting Ascension, to stand well to the westward for the Azores. Following this course, the JAVA touched at Madeira, where the officers and the Governor's suite laid in a stock of the native product. On Christmas Eve, being at the nearest point to Brazil on the well-known route, Captain Lambert had a report that water was short; the Governor and his suite had brought such an immensity of luggage that it was impossible to get at the water casks until the upper load was taken out of the ship. Captain Lambert then decided to put into Salvador to adjust cargo and take on water, but the two East Indiamen, feeling no need of further convoy, kept on their way. He was left with the WILLIAM, an American merchant ship he had captured on the way, putting into her a master's mate and nineteen seamen, whom he could ill spare.

On the 28th December, for the first time on the voyage, Captain Lambert ordered six broadsides of blank cartridge to be fired; for the majority of the crew it was the first time they had served a gun on ship-board. Next day, the 29th, at 2 a.m., the *Constitution* was seen, lying hove-to, a bad sign in those waters, where all shipping should be going about its business. Captain Lambert therefore parted with the WILLIAM, ordering her to go into Salvador while he examined the stranger, which was now seen to be making sail. In fact, it was supposed on board the *Constitution* that the JAVA was the expected *Essex*, and they kept approaching until, at about four miles away, the JAVA made the private recognition signals for British, Spanish or Portuguese ships, without reply; and the *Constitution* made the American one, without reply, and then wore ship away from the JAVA.

The JAVA was under a press of sail, and went in pursuit, definitely gaining in the chase; but the wind coming up quite strongly from the north-east, and the sea rising, she heeled so much that she had to take in her royals. On this, at 1.40 p.m., the *Constitution* also shortened sail, and hoisted her colours; the JAVA did the same, and they approached under the usual sail for fighting in moderate weather, top and top-gallant sails, one jib and the driver.

The action commenced at 2.10 p.m., with the *Constitution* firing a broadside at half a mile range, falling short; then, as the JAVA came close, another which whistled overhead; then the JAVA, ranging alongside within a few yards, gave a most effective broadside, which carried away the wheel, killed four men and wounded several more. The *Constitution* fired a third broadside, and under cover of the smoke wore away to lengthen the range. The JAVA followed, more broadsides were exchanged, and the *Constitution* again wore away. This time the JAVA passed close under her stern, in a most advantageous position for raking, but only one shot was fired; probably the inexperienced crew had not reloaded in time. The *Constitution* now had the weather-gauge, but this did not suit her tactics, so she made sail to leeward, giving the JAVA again the opportunity of crossing her stern, and this time giving her quite a raking broadside.

It was now 3 p.m., and the JAVA, with her raw crew, had given a very good account of herself; had for fifty minutes sustained the fire of an enormously superior opponent, and given as good as she got. Now, however, Commodore Bainbridge decided to close, and came alongside within forty yards, when the rapid fire of his well-served guns began to tell; the JAVA's rigging was cut to pieces, her masts badly damaged, and men were dropping every minute. Captain Lambert saw his serious disadvantage, and determined on boarding in a desperate attempt to save his ship; before the JAVA could be laid aboard of the enemy, however, the foremast came down with a terrific crash, smashing in the forecastle and blocking most of the deck. The *Constitution* now attained a commanding position on the JAVA's quarter, and poured in a tremendous fire of all arms, to which scarcely any reply could be given. At 3.30 p.m. Captain Lambert was mortally wounded by a musket-ball, and the command devolved upon Lieutenant Henry Ducie Chads, who was himself wounded but kept the deck. Still the pitiless fire continued; at 4 p.m. the mizzen-mast went, and from this or some other cause the ships fell away a little and lay broadside to broadside; immediately the men at the guns of the JAVA opened fire again, with the best broadsides they had given yet, although the flame from the guns was igniting the wreckage that hung overside. The *Constitution* now drew ahead to repair damages, and the crew of the JAVA cheered wildly, thinking she was retreating.

They were now set to work furiously, to get some sail on the wreck; a sail was rigged between the stump of the foremast and the remains of the bowsprit; a spare top-gallant mast was fished to the same stump, with a studding-sail set on it;

the mainmast could not stand in the heavy rolling, so it was cut away, and in the strong wind the JAVA began to make headway. Now, however, the *Constitution* began to come down, but the JAVA's men reloaded her guns with ball and grape-shot, and returned the fire defiantly. By 6 p.m. she had seventeen guns out of action, no spars left standing, all her boats destroyed, pumps disabled and the hull a mere piece of wreckage; when Lieutenant Chads ordered the colours to be hauled down. The raw, botched-together crew of the JAVA had acquitted themselves like veteran heroes; they had sustained a fight against fearful odds for four hours; they had 124 casualties killed and wounded; but they were ready to fight on when their commander put an end to the slaughter. Lieutenant Chads,* though wounded, remained on deck throughout the action; Boatswain Humble had his hand shot off, went below to have a tourniquet on the stump, and returned to the deck. 'I had my orders from Lieutenant Chads,' he explained simply, 'to cheer up the men with my pipe.'

The *Constitution* had 34 casualties killed and wounded, according to Commodore Bainbridge's account; but the British officers on board as prisoners estimated 52. She had several shot through her hull and masts, and of her eight boats only one could take the water. In this only boat Lieutenant Parker, first of the *Constitution*, boarded the *Java* and took possession; but had to send a message to the commodore that the ship was in a sinking condition and could not be salvaged. He was now ordered to remove all the prisoners and their baggage to the *Constitution*, and then set the *Java* on fire. With only one boat, the transfer was a tedious business, taking up the whole of the next day; but on the morning of the 31st January the *Java* was fired, and blew up about 3 p.m.

The officers of the *Constitution* have been criticised for the pressure brought to bear on the seamen prisoners to induce them to enter the American Navy; however, only three did so, believed to be Irish Roman Catholics, who had little cause to adhere faithfully to the British government. As the *Java* was about to blow up, one of these deserters informed the commodore that a large part of her cargo was gold bars, which he himself had helped to stow; Bainbridge's chagrin at this

* In 1824, Captain Henry Ducie Chads commanded the Irrawaddy flotilla during the Burmese War.

information may well be imagined, but after having enjoyed the ameliorations of the position for some time, the British officer prisoners were able to assure him that the precious metal was in fact copper.

Part of the prize was a very splendid service of silver, suited for the pomp and dignity of a Governor of Bombay; this Commodore Bainbridge ordered to be restored to Lieutenant-General Hislop, who returned the compliment with a present of a handsome sword. Captain Lambert died on the 4th January 1813, and was buried with full honours in Fort St Pedor, attended by the Governor of the fort, the Conde' dos Arcos. The American officers did not think it suitable to attend, but the commodore wrote to Lieutenant-General Hislop:

> Commodore Bainbridge has learned, with real sorrow, the death of Captain Lambert. Though a political enemy, he could not but greatly respect him for the brave defence he made with his ship; and Commodore Bainbridge takes this occasion to observe, in justice to Lieutenant Chads, who fought the JAVA after Captain Lambert was wounded, that he did everything for the defence of that ship that a brave and skilful officer could do, and that further resistance would have been a wanton effusion of human blood.

On the 6th of January 1813 Commodore Bainbridge decided that the damages to the *Constitution* were beyond local repair to fit her for a voyage round the Horn, and returned to Boston, where he was naturally received with rapture, a gold medal, the thanks of Congress supplemented with $50,000, silver medals for all the officers and a triumphal procession.

Commodore Bainbridge has been criticised (by a *very* partial British historian) for delaying the action so long, and indeed appearing to evade it; but it must be considered that he was at any moment expecting his consort the *Hornet* to come up, and at any hour the *Essex*. Before this formidable squadron it might be expected that the JAVA would surrender without further resistance, and allow him to resume his Pacific cruise; which, by engaging, he was forced to abandon. Indeed, it has to be observed that all these tactical victories of the big frigates were in fact strategical defeats; they had to abandon their main objective in every case. By running away from the *President* and consorts, the BELVIDERA saved the Jamaica convoy. By fighting the *United States*, the MACEDONIAN, although surrendered, caused that powerful ship to leave the track of the East India convoy and return to her home port; and by fighting the *Constitution* to the death, the JAVA turned her back from the Pacific, where her presence might have had very serious consequences. These defeats must be aligned with the defeat of the JERVIS BAY, Captain Fogarty Fegen, V.C., by the *Scheer*, Captain Krancke, on 5th November 1940. In all those cases the convoys were saved; the warships were lost: they had carried out their orders.

> *Go tell the Spartans, you that pass us by,*
> *Obedient to their orders, here we lie.*
> SIMONIDES, EPITAPH AT THERMOPYLAE.
> Author's trans.

14

Challenge Encounter

In England there was great dismay at the success of the big frigates in combat with British frigates of nominally nearly equal force; but Admiralty did not allow itself to attach too much importance to what was in fact a side-show. The whole American Navy was only a light squadron, compared with the powerful fleets which Napoleon had in the Scheldt, at Brest, at Rochefort, and at Toulon; the blockade of those fleets was recognised as the first business of the Royal Navy. It has been suggested that if Vice-Admiral Sir Edward Pellew, Bart., had been detached from Toulon with the lighter half of his fleet, the whole American business would have been settled in a few months. This is probably true, but the French fleet in Toulon was at least ten times more formidable than the whole American Navy, consisting of 21 ships of the line, 6 of them three-deckers, 3 of 130 guns each, plus 10 large frigates and all supporting craft, and several more building. To keep this immense force corked up in harbour was infinitely more important than odd frigate actions on the other side of the Atlantic.

Nevertheless, some action was taken. Three of the small class of 74-gun ships were cut down and lightened by having their quarter-decks and forecastles removed. Two new large and light ships were built of pitch pine, of about 1,560 tons, with powerful batteries. Any of these five was quite equal to any of the three big frigates; but in addition there were ordered twenty-six more large frigates, of the 36- and 38-gun classes, to be built of pine for speed and cheapness. The captains of frigates on the Halifax and Jamaica stations were ordered not to engage in single-ship actions with any of the big frigates, an order which almost caused a mutiny in one ship which ran away accordingly. The only thing Admiralty could not do was to provide them with good crews of seasoned sailors, and it must have been galling for the excellent officers of the new ships to man them with what was available, while in the Mediterranean there were twelve thousand fully trained prime seamen, hanging about hoping and praying that Vice-Admiral the Comte Emeriau would really come out and fight.

One ship that had no man-power problems was the 38-gun frigate SHANNON, Captain Philip Bowes Vere Broke, who took command on 14th September 1806 of a crew dragged aboard by the usual means; but by his skill as a seaman and a gunner, and by his outstanding personality as a leader of men, he shaped them into one of the best crews that ever trod a deck. Discipline was firm and impartial; sail drill and gunnery were more important than paint and polish; Broke spent his own money for extra powder, and gave a pound of tobacco to every gun that hit the mark. Seven years he spent in training his men, and by that time every man knew exactly what he was required to do, and how to do it; he had done it often before.

In 1813, on the Halifax station, Captain Broke found himself the senior captain, under Rear-Admiral Sawyer. There was a bit of two-and-fro squadron demonstrations, but eventually Broke found an objective in May 1813, the *Chesapeake*, completing repairs in Boston Harbour. She was a frigate of equal or slightly greater force than the SHANNON, well manned, and commanded by Captain Lawrence, who had earlier had a successful cruise in command of the *Hornet*, sloop. The *Constitution* was also in the harbour, but having an extensive repair and alteration, so that she was not to be ready for sea for some months. Broke had with him the TENEDOS, 38-gun frigate, Captain Hyde Parker; Broke now took some supplies out of the TENEDOS, and sent her away, with orders not to come within reach of Boston before 14th June, as it was obvious that the *Chesapeake* could not be expected to come out to fight two to one.

Thinking that the *Chesapeake* was somewhat tardy, Broke now sent in a formal written challenge to Lawrence, by a captured American merchantman, Captain Slocum, surely an ancestor of Captain Joshua Slocum, the first single-handed circumnavigator.

'As the *Chesapeake* appears now ready for sea, I request you will do me the favour to meet the SHANNON with her, ship to ship, to try the fortune of our respective flags.' He goes on to detail precisely the armament and complement of his ship, and promises that there will be no interruption by any British ship, concluding with a request for a speedy reply. As a matter of fact, Captain Lawrence was just as ready for a meeting as Broke, but he had to get permission from Commodore Bainbridge, who had had to get permission from Washington, which was forthcoming; and Lawrence did not ever receive this faintly medieval invitation to come out and be killed. This is probably the very last formal challenge between warships. Before Slocum reached the shore, the *Chesapeake* was making sail, and shortly after noon was seen standing out from the harbour under easy sail, accompanied by a perfect regatta of small craft filled with spectators, including, it is believed, two commodores and some other officers. The wind was light from west by north, and the SHANNON now stood away from the shore, not wishing to engage surrounded by all those boats, which would certainly be a nuisance and possibly might conceal a menace. The *Chesapeake* followed under all sail, which she shortened at 4.50 p.m. At 5.30 the SHANNON shortened sail to battle rig, Boston lighthouse then being about twenty miles to the westward. *Chesapeake* now came up, and having the weather-gauge could either engage on the weather side, or pass under the SHANNON's stern, rake her with a broadside and then engage on the lee side. Captain Broke had provided for both possibilities; the *Chesapeake* chose to keep the weather side, and came along quite slowly at a range of about fifty yards.

This was the moment the SHANNON had been training for, through seven years. A.B. William Mindham, gun-captain of the aftermost starboard 18-pounder, knew his orders; to wait until his gun could bear on the second gunport from forward of the enemy; at 5.50 p.m. he fired the first shot of the action, hitting his objective with two round shot and a keg of musket balls. Now the rest of the guns fired in succession as they came to bear, and as the *Chesapeake* passed, the 32-pounder carronades on the quarter-deck of the SHANNON swept her quarter-deck with grape-shot as well as round-shot. The *Chesapeake* now fired her broadside, which was answered; and as the *Chesapeake* was running too far ahead, her main-top sail was backed, to take the way off her. Unfortunately the men at the wheel were all killed or wounded by the fire from the SHANNON's quarter-deck, so that the *Chesapeake* continued to swing into the wind, losing all way, thus presenting her quarter-deck and quarter to the raking fire of the SHANNON, to which little reply could be given. The *Chesapeake* now began to drift astern, and fell on board the SHANNON, with the larboard corner of her stern against the starboard side of the SHANNON, a little forward of the mainmast. This check swung the *Chesapeake* more into the wind, and her foresail began to take up, although damaged, and she moved ahead slowly, rubbing along the SHANNON's hull, until she hooked on to the SHANNON's small bower-anchor.

Captain Broke now ordered the ships to be lashed together, First Lieutenant Watts to get together the quarter-deck men for boarding, and the main deck boarders to be ordered up, while he himself ran forward to take command of the forecastle boarders, whose leader, midshipman Samwell, was mortally wounded. The lashing together of the ships was done by Mr Stevens, the SHANNON's veteran boatswain, who had fought in the battle of the Sainte's Passage thirty-two years before, 'when Rodney beat the Comte de Grasse'. Mr Stevens was assailed by the defenders as he worked, and his left arm was hacked off by repeated cutlass-strokes, but he finished his job with his right hand before he was shot down by musketry.*

Captain Broke now stepped over the gangway railing, around the foremast rigging, on to the muzzle of the *Chesapeake*'s aftermost quarter-deck carronade, and threw himself over the bulwark, followed immediately by the forecastle party of about twenty men. They found the quarter-deck clear of all except dead and wounded, but about thirty men on the gangways. A fierce charge drove these back to the forecastle, where after a brief struggle some (no doubt British deserters) jumped over the bows into the sea, while the others laid down their

---

* Parallels almost as precise are to be found in Cynaegeirus after Marathon, under Miltiades and Caius Acilius, in the battle off Marseilles, under Julius Caesar. Such devotion to duty is seldom to be found except among the followers of the great captains.

arms and surrendered. Meanwhile the enemy tried to regain the quarter-deck by coming up the main hatch; but First Lieutenant Watts was already there, with the quarter-deck boarders and a division of the Marines, who were followed by the main deck boarders and more Marines. Lieutenant Watts was shot through the foot while boarding, but remained in command on the *Chesapeake*'s quarter-deck. The shot came from the American Marines in the main and mizzen tops, and it was the duty of the small parties in the SHANNON's tops to deal with this. Midshipman William Smith, in the fore-top, observed that the main-yard of the *Chesapeake* was in contact with the fore-yard over which was his fighting-top. Waiting until the Marines opposite had fired a volley and were reloading, he swarmed along both yards with his four men and cleared the *Chesapeake*'s top with the cutlass. The *Chesapeake*'s mizzen-top was silenced and cleared by Midshipman Cosnahan, from the main-top of the SHANNON; a good shot, he kept his four men loading muskets, enabling him to keep up a rapid and accurate fire which killed or wounded all the American Marines in the mizzen-top; they used rifles, which at that time took three times as long to load as a musket, which was as accurate at twenty yards.

Boatswain Stevens' tackle held; but the quarter-deck gallery of the *Chesapeake*, to which he had made fast, now fetched away, and the two ships began slowly to drift apart. On the forecastle of the *Chesapeake* Captain Broke, setting a single sentry over the prisoners, directed the rest of his boarders to return to the quarter-deck where fierce fighting was engaged. While casting his captain's eye round the ship, he was alerted by a shout from the sentry. The prisoners had picked up their weapons and resumed fighting, the first casualty being the sentry, immediately after he had warned his captain. Broke was now attacked by several men: he parried a thrust from a pike, and wounded the pikeman; but was stunned by a blow from the butt-end of a musket, and cut down by a blow from a cutlass; this assailant was in the act of swinging his cutlass to finish off the wounded captain, when, with a rush and a roar, the main deck boarders charged along the gangways. William Mindham, that accurate gun-captain, cut down and killed Broke's adversary, while the rest of the main deck boarders cleared the forecastle in one furious assault. No quarter was given, as was indeed justified by the laws of war, but it is doubtful if the seamen stopped to debate the legal point; their blood was up, and they had seen their captain fall.

Midshipman Smith, who had just cleared the main-top, came down to the deck and helped A.B. Mindham to get Broke to his feet. While they were bandaging his head as best they could, Mindham cried: 'There, Sir, there goes the old Ensign up over the Yankee colours!' Immediately Captain Broke was helped to the quarter-deck, where he was seated on a carronade-slide, in command of the CHESAPEAKE.

An unfortunate accident, however, had marred the changing of the colours, Lieutenant Watts himself hauled down the American flag, and hauled them up again, with, as he thought, the British ensign above it. He had been better to have left the job to a signal rating, for he had somehow got the toggles mixed and the colours went up with the Ensign underneath. The ships had by this time drifted about a hundred yards apart, and the quarter-deck gunners of the SHANNON, seeing through the smoke these colours, judged that the ship had been re-taken and fired a broadside, which killed their own first lieutenant and four of their shipmates. Their chagrin and regret may be imagined, but they were doing their duty in the circumstances. After the colours were hoisted correctly, some Americans in the hold of the ship fired up, killing a Marine; Lieutenant Falkiner, third of the SHANNON, ordered his men to fire into the hold, which they did with effect. Captain Broke ordered Lieutenant Falkiner to cease fire, and to ask the men in the hold if they surrendered; no quarter if they wanted to carry on the fight. They surrendered and all fighting ceased. The ship was not formally surrendered, for there was not a single commissioned officer left on his feet to offer his sword. The SHANNON's jolly-boat came alongside with reinforcements just as Captain Broke fainted from loss of blood, and the jolly-boat took him back to the SHANNON.

This was one of the shortest actions of the wars. From the first gun until the changing of the colours only fifteen minutes elapsed—roughly, eleven for the cannonade and four for the boarding action. It was also one of the fiercest—in that quarter of an hour 229 men had been struck down, many never to rise. The SHANNON had 24 killed and 59 wounded, some mortally; but the *Chesapeake* had 47 killed and 99 wounded, 14 mortally. Her casualties included all her commissioned officers; captain and first lieutenant mortally wounded, second and third lieutenants wounded, fourth lieutenant killed, lieutenant of Marines killed.

Lieutenant Provo Wallis, second of the SHANNON, now took command of her, while the third, Lieutenant Falkiner, took the CHESAPEAKE; on the 6th of June 1813, they arrived at Halifax to great acclamation. Captain Lawrence died during the voyage, and was buried at Halifax with full military honours of his rank; Lieutenant Ludlow died after arrival, and was similarly buried; but a cartel later was given the remains for burial in their own country. Both Lieutenants Wallis and Falkiner were promoted to be commanders, and Wallis was commissioned to take the CHESAPEAKE to Portsmouth.

This battle excited the greatest excitement in Britain, and with good cause. The history of the naval war with America had up till now been an unbroken succession of defeats, which might be explained away but were undoubted defeats; was the sceptre of the seas slipping from the hand of Britannia? Now, in a straight fight between ships of equal force the British had been decisively successful. There were, too, touches about it which stirred the imagination, touches reminiscent of the days of chivalry. The formal challenge—the heroic devotion of the boatswain—the Captain leading the first wave of boarders—the Captain engaged single-handed in a three-to-one close combat—the young midshipman storming the enemy fighting-top along the yard-arms—the fierce combat on the enemy deck: here were all the elements of romance.

Captain Broke was made a Baronet for this engagement, but owing to his wounds and the war ending he did not serve again, dying fairly young as a rear-admiral. Very different was the later career of his second lieutenant. Provo Wallis was not made post captain, which he might have expected after commanding a frigate, if only for a few weeks; but he got post rank in 1819. Now all he had to do was to survive, and he had emerged unscathed from his only engagement so that there were no old wounds to worry about. He kept on steadily up the captains' ladder, and then up the admirals' ladder; until in 1877 he became Admiral of the Fleet, and moreover enjoyed that rank and pay for nearly fifteen years, dying in 1892, age 100. He was an institution, especially as he retained all his faculties and replied with his own hand to all the congratulations on his hundredth birthday. To a nation proud of its fleet, equal to all the navies in the world together; in those days of twelve-inch armour, steam propulsion, and 81-ton guns; here was a man who could tell how he had fought ship to ship under sail in the wooden walls, eighty years before.

15

South Pacific

Somewhat elated by the early successes of their big frigates, the government of the U.S.A. decided to put a squadron into the South Pacific, where no American warship had formerly made an appearance. The ships chosen were the *Constitution*, one of the extra-large frigates, the *Hornet*, a sloop, and the *Essex*, a small frigate of 867 tons, but with a very powerful close-range battery, having forty carronades, 32-pounders, and six long 12-pounders. Sailing from different ports, the three were to rendezvous off Salvador (Bahia) on the coast of Brazil. While waiting around there, the *Constitution* met the British frigate JAVA, and after a fierce fight captured and sank her; but was so much damaged that she had to return to a home port for repairs, accompanied by the *Hornet* (Chapter 13). When the *Essex* arrived and found no consorts, Captain David Porter decided to make the cruise alone, and arrived at Valparaiso on the 14th of March 1813, having captured by the way a British packet-ship out of which he took £11,000 in coin. Here he refitted the *Essex* after the stormy passage round Cape Horn, took in provisions and water, and set off to cruise in the whaling-grounds of the South Seas.

On receiving this intelligence Admiralty sent in pursuit the 36-gun 18-pounder frigate PHOEBE, Captain James Hillyard, who had been doing good service in the Indian Ocean, along with the 18-gun ship-sloop CHERUB, Commander Thomas Tucker. At first sight it seems quite ludicrous to send two ships to find one ship in the vast emptiness of the great South Seas; but the task was not as impossible as might appear. If the *Essex* were going to prey on the whale-fishing, which was probable, she must keep in the vicinity where the whale-ships were accustomed to go, for water, provisions and careening; and the eastern South Pacific has very few such places; it is the only stretch of water in the world where it is possible to be more than a thousand miles from the very nearest scrap of land.

After rounding the Horn Captain Hillyard made for Juan Fernandez, where he got no news; then to Guayaquil on the Ecuador coast—still no news; then to the Galapagos Islands, where he learned that the *Essex* had been there in October with some captured whale-ships, one of which, the ATLANTIC, he had renamed the *Essex Junior* and armed with twenty guns. Where now? It was probable that Captain Porter would try to sell his prizes on the coast of South America, for the chances of getting them home through the blockade were remote. Captain Hillyard therefore went to Lima, where he waited two months without any news.

Actually at that time the *Essex* was at Nuka Hiva, one of the Marquesas islands, nearly five thousand miles away, where Porter remained until 12th December 1813, cleaning ships and dealing with his twelve captures. One of these he had armed as described, and manned with a crew of ninety-five men; two he gave over to the prisoners, having taken the oil into the other prizes. One he armed with sixteen guns, and sent her off to the U.S.A. with two others, all fully laden; they were all captured by the frigates in the Atlantic. Three were burnt at sea. One was taken by the CHERUB, and one was seized by her prize crew and taken to Sydney Harbour. This leaves one not accounted for, possibly sold in Chile, possibly lost at sea.

The *Essex* and the *Essex Junior* with two of the prizes now sailed for Valparaiso, where they arrived in January 1814, hoping to sell their prizes. It is possible that the *Montezuma*, the one not accounted for, was sold on this occasion, but there were no bidders for the *Hector*, the other one; rumours of a British force on the coast made it a perilous speculation. In fact Captain Hillyard had tired of waiting in Lima for news, and coasted south; rounding the point of the harbour of Valparaiso, he found what he had been seeking for the last nine months.

The rules about belligerent ships in neutral waters were less well defined in those days, and were further complicated by the fact that Chile, as a Spanish colony, was now an ally of Britain in the war against France, but neutral in the American war on Britain. As usual, much depended on what force was available. Both sides, therefore, called their men to quarters, without, however, clearing for action. The PHOEBE came in very close to the *Essex*, and, according to a letter written a little later by a midshipman who was on the quarter-deck at the time, Captain Hillyard hailed Captain Porter to ask if he was well (they were old acquaintances). Captain Porter returned the compliment, but added, 'If the PHOEBE touches the *Essex* there will be serious consequences.' 'Upon my honour, I do not mean to touch you, I respect the neutrality of the port, and only came alongside to inquire after your health.' Captain Porter replied, 'Excuse me, Captain Hillyard, in calling my boarders', to which Hillyard replied, 'I thought you knew me better, Sir, than to think I would break my word —you have no occasion to be so much alarmed.' 'I am *not* alarmed, Sir—stand by, my boys!' On this the crew of the *Essex* manned her side and rigging, fully armed to repel boarders; the PHOEBE did the same, and passing on in this state of readiness came to anchor quite close. In the same way the CHERUB anchored almost alongside the *Essex Junior*, and the crews spent most of the night shouting insults at each other.

At 8 a.m. next morning, along with the usual colours the *Essex* hoisted a large white flag at the fore top-gallant masthead, bearing the motto 'Free Trade and Sailors' Rights'. It was known that a number of British sailors out of the captured whalers had been persuaded to enter into American service in the *Essex* on some such grounds, 'sailors' rights' being interpreted as meaning rum without ration. The PHOEBE now prepared and hoisted a counter-blast, 'God and country, British sailors' best Rights, Traitors offend both'. While these childish demonstrations were going on, the PHOEBE and CHERUB were taking in provisions, wood and water; when this was completed they stood out to cruise about in the bay, while the Americans remained moored in the anchorage.

The PHOEBE, in addition to her main battery of twenty-six long 18-pounders, carried fourteen carronades, 32-pounders, and four long 9-pounders on her quarter-deck and forecastle. She was thus somewhat lighter in weight of broadside than the *Essex*, with the vital difference that almost the whole of the battery of the *Essex* was in carronades. She had therefore little chance against the PHOEBE, which in open sea conditions could keep out of carronade range and hammer the *Essex* into surrender with her long 18s. At close quarters it would be different, but the CHERUB carried eighteen carronades, 32-pounders, as well as six 18-pounder carronades and two long 6s, so that in 32-pounder carronades the *Essex* was out-gunned by two, and there were still the twenty-six 18-pounders in the PHOEBE. The *Essex Junior* was not constructed as a war-ship and had only ten each 18-pounder carronades and 6-pounder long guns; quite hopeless against the CHERUB. The plan therefore was to get away rather than fight in such cir-cumstances. The usual wind in that area being from the south, Captain Porter decided to try to decoy the British ships to the northern coast of the shore, slip out himself and let them chase him, fighting if he must, to give the *Essex Junior* a fair chance of escape. In case both got away, the rendezvous was fixed for Nuka Hiva.

Some weeks passed in futile manœuvres. On the 25th Feb-ruary Captain Porter had his prize the *Hector* towed out of port and burnt. On the night of the 27th of March Captain Porter sent a small party to the north shore of the bay to burn blue-lights and shoot off rockets, to attract the British ships in that direction. This was partially successful, but at daylight the PHOEBE was still too close to the mouth of the port for an attempt at escape. A strong wind began to blow from the SSE and increased so much that the *Essex* dragged her starboard anchor. Seizing the opportunity, Captain Porter ordered the other cable to be cut and sail made. The *Essex* reached the mouth of the harbour well to windward of her opponents exactly as Captain Porter had planned, but just as she emerged to the open sea a still stronger squall carried away her main topmast, and with it all hope of escape. The *Essex* bore up, and after running before the wind for some time came to an anchor in a small bay. Between 3.30 and 4 p.m. the PHOEBE crossed the stern of the *Essex*, at a greater distance than was intended, and gave some raking broadsides, while the CHERUB also opened fire. The *Essex* replied with three of her long 12-pounders, which the crew had managed to run out of her stern-ports. After half an hour of this long-range firing, the British ships were too near the shore and had to wear away for sea-room. They had by no means had the best of this brief encounter. The PHOEBE had a 12-pound shot through her hull well below the waterline, and was much damaged in the rigging, as was also the CHERUB. After about an hour the wind fell almost to a calm, and the PHOEBE once more approached the *Essex*, this time much closer. After about twenty minutes of fierce cannonade the *Essex* cut her cable and tried to run on shore, but a sudden squall from off the mountains (a 'williwaw') drove her right back again; she again anchored about three-quarters of a mile off shore, but this left her in a hopeless position, with her stern exposed to the fire of both the British ships' broadsides.

The *Essex* had gone into action with many ensigns flying, but the cannonade had left only one, which she now hauled down; 'but,' says our midshipman, 'kept *Free Trade*, etc. flying, so we gave her several more broadsides before she sent a man up to haul this flag down, but a shot took him, flag and all, just as he was in the act of striking it and so put an end to the business.'

Now was seen the extraordinary sight of about a hundred men leaping from the deck of the *Essex* into the sea. These were the British seamen who had been induced to join the *Essex* out of the captured whalers, and who now realised the full meaning of the word 'traitors' on the flag the PHOEBE was still flying. The non-swimmers crowded into the only boat the *Essex* had left, in such numbers that the boat swamped and left them struggling hopelessly in the water. Of the rest, about 40 reached the shore, about 30 drowned, and 16 were taken from the water by the boats of the British ships.

'I was in the 1st boat that boarded her,' wrote our midshipman. 'Nothing was to be seen all over her decks but dead, wounded and dying—we threw 63 overboard that were dead and there were several wounded that it would have been a mercy to do the same to . . . One poor fellow, who had his thigh shot off, managed to crawl to a port and tumble himself into the water which put an end to his misery. There were 44 amputations performed that night . . . Captain Porter was in tears when he went on board the PHOEBE to give up his sword and he told Captain Hillyard that there were 15 of his brave fellows killed after she struck.'

The loss sustained by the *Essex* has been the subject of

much controversy. Captain Porter gives it as 58 killed and mortally wounded, 39 severely and 27 slightly wounded. This tallies not badly with the account given by our young eyewitness, and is quite consonant with the expectable loss of a heavily manned ship which had been exposed stern-on to broadsides from a total of 33 guns and carronades, 18-pounders and over, for two hours. The official letter of Captain Hillyard says 'The defence of the *Essex* . . . did honour to her brave defenders, and most fully evinced the courage of Captain Porter, and those under his command. Her colours were not struck until the loss in killed and wounded was so awfully great, and her shattered condition so seriously bad, as to render further resistance unavailing.' Well, there is the testimony of three who were there; but respectable historians, who were not there, have reduced the loss figures to less than half, for reasons it is difficult to follow; and indeed if the first boat-load of British to take over the ship began by throwing the dead overboard, an accurate count is not to be expected.

The loss of the PHOEBE was 4 killed and 7 wounded, and of the CHERUB 1 killed and 3 wounded. Captain Hillyard has been criticised (mostly by American writers) for taking too long and fighting at a fair distance; but if he had thrown away the only advantage his ship had, and had fought within point-blank carronade range of the forty 32-pounders of the *Essex*, he would have deserved to be cashiered. A good captain will take every fair advantage open to him, and will save his men as far as he possibly can.

16

Shipwreck

After the general settlement of Europe after Waterloo, the British government determined to send an Embassy to the Emperor of China, to inform him officially of the events and settlement, to profess the friendship of the British Crown, and to convey to him a very splendid service of silver. For this important office the choice fell on Lord Amherst, a very able peer, who was later to be Governor of Canada and later still Governor-General of India. He was naturally consulted about the transport he wished, and he asked for the frigate ALCESTE, commanded by his friend Captain Murray Maxwell.

The ALCESTE and her captain had already distinguished themselves in the wars, chiefly in the Adriatic, where one action may have changed the course of history. The ALCESTE, along with the ACTIVE, Captain James Gordon, and the 36-gun UNITÉ, Captain Edwin Chamberlayne, was lying at Lissa when they were informed of a French squadron, almost identical, sailing northwards. The British immediately chased, and after a fierce encounter captured two of the French frigates, the third making its escape. This was a splendid feat of war, but what made it more interesting was the fact that the captured frigates were laden with more than two hundred guns, with the carriages and all necessary stores, bound for Trieste. This action took place on 28th November 1811, and the news of it may have made Napoleon realise that he could never build up Illyria as a springboard against Turkey. After all, he deployed only 250 guns at Waterloo, so the loss of 200 was indeed serious. Thus it may well be that Murray Maxwell's minor victory may have been the last factor that made

Napoleon abandon at that time his designs on Constantinople, and go to Moscow instead.

As well as being one of the finest 38-gun frigates in the Royal Navy, assiduous in all duties and terrible in action, the ALCESTE was a happy ship. One who served in her, on the lower deck, described her as the happiest home he ever had. Murray Maxwell was the ideal captain; his personality was such that his whole crew hero-worshipped him; he had no need to use the lash; the mere idea of displeasing him was sufficient discipline. The men admired him for his seamanship and skill, and his complete intrepidity in battle; and they loved him for his impartiality and his firm and kindly command. There could be no better choice of a ship for a long, hazardous and important voyage than the ALCESTE.

The outward voyage was accomplished without particular incident, and the ALCESTE lay at Whampoa, the usual anchorage for Canton, while the Ambassador and his suite carried out their duties at the Imperial Court. They were received with the usual ceremonies, but did not make the impression they expected. The Celestial Emperor indicated that he had little interest in the squabbles of distant barbarians, and declined the present of plate, on the grounds that he had no use for it, using only gold or jade himself. *Timeo Danaos et dona ferentes* was his view, and a very sound one in his case. The Embassy returned to Canton, having accomplished as much of their mission as they could, only embarrassed about what to do with the service of plate. Obviously the Prince Regent could not receive it back again. In the long run, after various vicissitudes, it was sold by auction at Calcutta, and purchased by a Mr Hawkins, who had accumulated a vast fortune, no doubt honestly, as Agent at Bareilly for the Governor-General, and he produced it when he entertained General Lord Combermore, the Commander-in-Chief, and his suite during his Excellency's Simla progress in December 1828.

The ALCESTE sailed from Whampoa on the 21st of January 1817, having on board 257 persons, including the Ambassador and his suite, so that she would appear to be somewhat undermanned. No doubt before leaving England some guns had been put ashore, to make more accommodation room, so that fewer hands would be required. The course was through the South China Seas, for the Sunda Strait between Sumatra and

Java, whence there is a clear run, with mostly favourable winds, to Cape Town.

The South China Sea is the most dangerous water in all the oceans. Even today there is a great area, about 100,000 square miles, west of Palawan, which has never been surveyed; some reefs and rocks round the perimeter have been marked, the rest called 'The Dangerous Area' and left at that. From Bangkok to Java is 1,500 miles, nowhere deeper than 40 fathoms, and in those shallow waters the frequent typhoons can whip up a fearsome short steep sea. Moreover, from the shallows rise hundreds of shoals, islands and sunken reefs, many of which are so steep-to that the sounding-line, and even the echo-sounder, can give no warning of their proximity.

Having chosen the season with care, the ALCESTE had favourable winds throughout the passage, and twenty-eight days out was approaching the last hazard before the Sunda Straits. Nowadays ships use the Gaspar Strait, between the small island of Liat and the large island of Belitung; but at that time the known channel was the Bangka Strait, between the large island of Bangka and the west coast of Liat. It may be assumed that every precaution was taken, and certainly the sounding-line was kept going continuously throughout the passage, but she struck with terrific force upon a sunken and uncharted reef, where she stuck fast.

Everyone on board was as cool as the captain, who ordered the sails to be furled and the best bower anchor let go, to prevent the ship slipping off the reef until the state of damage could be ascertained. Mr Cheffy, the carpenter, now reported that the water was coming in much faster than all the pumps could cope with, that the damage to the hull underwater was beyond repair, and if she came off into deep water she would immediately sink; in fact, she was a total loss.

The captain's first care was for the Ambassador, the King's Representative. An island was seen about three miles away. The barge and cutter were put under command of the First Lieutenant, Hopper, who was ordered to convey the Ambassador and suite to the island, and land them there if it seemed safe. They made the island, which appeared to be uninhabited but heavily forested; they had to coast for three more miles before they found an opening in the mangroves, and were able to land their passengers, after which they returned to the ship. Meanwhile the remaining boats had been hoisted out, and a large raft constructed, on which were placed the articles too large to be stowed in the boats. All that could be reached in the way of food, water, arms and tools was stowed in the boats, which made for the landing-place with the whole ship's company, towing the raft. On landing, a space was cleared under the nearest trees, where all the castaways bivouacked for the night.

In the morning, on taking stock, it was found that the most immediate shortage was water; one small cask, and a jar in the barge, was the whole stock. Parties were now sent out in various directions, but returned having found no water. After a council, it was decided that the first lieutenant should convey Lord Amherst and his suite to Batavia (now Djakarta) in Java, which lay a little more than two hundred miles to the southward, using the same boats which had brought them ashore. Given fair weather, the voyage should be easily done in four days; but of course the weather might not stay fair. On arrival, Lord Amherst was immediately to send a relief ship. There was very little prospect of sighting a passing vessel, as the Company's ships which used the Sunda Strait continued eastward for Java and the Spice Islands, while those bound for China sailed from Calcutta using the Singapore Strait 350 miles to the north. For food they had a side of mutton, a ham, a tongue, twenty pounds of coarse biscuit and a few pounds of fine; and for drink a seven-gallon jar each of water, beer, and spruce beer, and thirty bottles of wine. For four days this was a pint of liquid per man per day, a very meagre allowance when it is considered that all their provisions were either salt meat or dry biscuit, and they were in latitude 3° south of the equator. However, the men left behind were in worse case; so the boats rowed out well clear of all the rocks, and then made sail and were soon below the horizon.

The party on the island numbered two hundred men and boys, and one woman, turned up, as usual, from nowhere. The water-cask saved from the ship would afford one pint per head for two days only, while it must be at the very best nine days before relief could arrive. Water was the first consideration. The Captain made a quick survey to decide a likely spot, and set a party to digging a well. Another party was sent on board the wreck, to get by what means they could as much provision and arms they might reach. Captain Maxwell decided to remove the bivouac to the top of a small hill, for better air and for defence, and he set a party to cut a path and to clear away the undergrowth at the top. A sort of cave near the top formed a cool larder, where the provisions were stowed, and a Marine guard posted. In short, everything was done to prepare for an indefinite stay on the island.

The great interest was the well, where digging went on continuously. At eleven at night the diggers were twenty feet down, where they came across a layer of clay, into which there appeared to be a slight seepage. A little after midnight a bottle of muddy water was brought to the captain, who pronounced it to be fresh. This caused such a rush to the well that the captain posted a guard to allow the diggers to get on with their work, at the same time proclaiming that no water would be served out until there was an equal ration for everybody. At that moment there commenced a heavy fall of rain, which was collected as well as possible in sails and sheets, and gave everybody at least a mouthful, while the well-diggers completed their work by sinking a cask into the clay and lining the shaft with wood. Before noon the next day, the 20th February, every man had a pint of fresh water, tasting slightly of coconut, and the well was filling at a rate which promised at least two pints a day. The most dreaded of all calamities was averted.

At dawn next day the party on board the wreck found themselves surrounded by several Malay proas, some with swivels mounted in their bows, filled with about eighty Malays, well armed with spears and krises. As the wreck-party had no weapon of any kind, all they could do was to get into their boat and pull for the shore, pursued by the Malays. This was observed from the shore, and two boats with armed parties pushed out, on which the Malays gave over and returned to the wreck. Shortly a look-out reported that two proas were landing armed men at a point about two miles from the encampment. It was at once assumed that they intended to attack, as it was well known that when these sea-Dyaks took a ship they invariably murdered everybody on board, and indeed some tribes were suspected of cannibalism, not improbable in those protein-starved rain-forest islands. Captain

Maxwell therefore ordered all other activity to cease, and to prepare for defence.

A party under Mr Cheffy, the carpenter, felled the remaining trees on the hill-top and made an open stockade around the area. The boys were set to cutting saplings and branches and weaving them into the uprights, making a tolerable breastwork which would give some protection and certainly prevent a rush assault. Stock was taken of weapons; the Marines had thirty muskets and bayonets, but only seventy-five ball cartridges amongst them. The gunner, however, had drawn the charges from the quarter-deck carronades before leaving the ship, so that there was about a hundred pounds of loose coarse powder and some horns of fine for the pans; broken bottles supplied the place of shot. Spear-shafts were made from branches and saplings, and knives, chisels and ship-nails were fixed to the ends; when these ran out, sharpening the end of the shaft and hardening it in the fire made a good enough weapon for a stout arm. There were about a dozen cutlasses. When the breastwork was complete, and all hands mustered, every man had some sort of weapon and the determination to use it.

A scouting party now returned, and reported that the pirates had not actually landed on the island, but on some off-lying rocks, which they were using as a depository for their plunder from the wreck. Every precaution was nevertheless taken against a night attack. Parties were set to guard the boats and the well, and inside the stockade the men were arranged in their divisions, each with a place allotted in the event of an alarm.

Next morning, the 22nd February, some Malay boats approached the landing-place, and an officer went out to them, waving a green bough; they made no response to this overture, however, but returned to the rock. Captain Maxwell perceived that the pirates were now in two separated bodies, and ordered Second Lieutenant Hay (the first having gone to Batavia) to take three boats and a well-armed boarding party and attempt to regain possession of the wreck. As the boats approached, those on the rock threw their plunder into their proas and made sail away. There were two large proas at the ship, and these also made off; but first they set fire to the ship so efficiently that the boats were unable to board her, and returned to shore. This was no calamity, however, for Captain Maxwell had already made up his mind to burn her, so that when the upperworks and decks were destroyed it would be possible for stores to float up from below. What the Malays chiefly wanted were nails and copper and any kind of metalwork, which was of no interest to the castaways, so that if contact had been made some sort of accommodation might have been arranged, but this was not possible with such ferocious and suspicious savages. The ship burned all night, the flames lighting the shore, casting odd shadows, so that a sentry fired on a baboon which failed to answer his challenge. This was quite a good exercise, however, for instantly after the shot every man was at his station.

In the morning, while the captain took the Service, two boats were sent to the smouldering wreck and returned with some barrels of flour, cases of wine, and—cheers!—a cask of beer; so that everybody had a Sunday pint. The lookout reported that most of the Malays had gone no further than an islet two miles away, but some had made sail apparently for Belitung. This suggested that they had sent for reinforcements, so all efforts were made to improve the position by cutting trees and burning undergrowth outside the stockade, to strengthen the work and to clear a field of fire. At the same time every effort was made to secure more ammunition and provisions from the wreck.

Nothing more was seen of the pirates until first light on Wednesday the 26th, when two proas with canoes astern were seen stealing into the cove where the boats were moored. Lieutenant Hay, who had the night watch, immediately sallied at them with his boats, on which the Malays cut their canoes adrift and made sail away. The boat with Hay overtook one of them, which fired its swivels without hitting anything, and the boat's crew boarded; four of the pirates were killed in a short desperate struggle, five jumped overboard and were not seen again, and two were taken prisoner. The proa would have been a useful prize, but the Malays had scuttled her and she sank almost immediately.

Later that morning fourteen more proas appeared, and anchored off the islet two miles off; one appeared to be much larger than the others, and to carry some rajah or other magnate. This gave rise to some hopes of a treaty, but the next day, the 27th, the rajah was observed superintending the plundering of the wreck, which went on for the next few days. Meantime Captain Maxwell had his boats moved to another and safer cove, where two little fortlets were erected on rocks which covered the entrance. On the 1st of March fourteen more proas arrived, and during that night several more were observed, but too indistinctly to count them. Next morning, while a number surrounded the wreck, twenty of the largest vessels approached the landing place, and anchored in a line about a cable from the shore; firing their swivels, beating gongs, and altogether making a most belligerent display. They did not yet attempt a landing, but it seemed certain that they were only waiting for nightfall.

At divisions that evening Captain Maxwell made his men a speech. 'My lads, you must all have observed the great increase in the enemy's force, and the threatening posture they have assumed. I have reason to believe they will attack us this night. I do not wish to conceal our real state, because I do not think there is a man here who is afraid to face any sort of danger. We are in a position to defend ourselves against regular troops, far less a set of naked savages, with their spears and krises. It is true they have swivels in their boats, but they cannot act here. I have not observed that they have any muskets, but if they have, so have we. When we were first thrown on shore we could only muster seventy-five ball cartridges—we have now sixteen hundred. They cannot send up, I believe, more than five hundred men; but with two hundred such as now stand around me, I do not fear a thousand —nor fifteen hundred of them. The pikemen standing firm, we shall give them such a volley of musketry as they will be little prepared for; and when they are thrown into confusion, we will sally out, chase them into the water, and ten to one but we secure their vessels. Let every man be on the alert, and should these barbarians this night attempt our hill, I trust we shall convince them that they are dealing with Britons.'

The loud cheers with which this harangue was received may have had a deterrent effect on the pirates, for the expected attack was not made. They retained their position, however, and next morning, 3rd March, it was observed that ten more proas had joined during the night. The situation now began to look gloomy; the relief ship was long overdue, and the feeling was that the boats with Lord Amherst must have come to grief; provisions were running down, while the strength of the enemy was continually growing. In such circumstances, it appeared that the only thing was to make a night attack with the four boats, capture some proas, man them also and try to capture more, so as to get enough shipping to take the whole company to Batavia. The raft was obviously of no use, as towing it would make movement very slow, and men on it would be exposed to the fire of the swivels on the proas, whereas in the boats and captured proas they would be at least as fast as the enemy and well able to defend themselves with musketry. The general idea was for two boats to attack one proa; this would give two proas, and while the boarding parties were taking them the crews would row ashore for more.

Detailed orders for this desperate attempt were being prepared, when the look-out reported a sail at a great distance to the south. A passing squall concealed it from sight, and some thought that the look-out had mistaken the forward streamers of the squall for a sail; however, an experienced signalman was sent up with a telescope, and in about half an hour he was able to assert that it was a square-rigged vessel, either a ship or a brig, standing directly for the island. Shortly the pirates also, from their lower position, saw the approaching sail, which caused some consternation among them. Captain Maxwell now ordered almost all the company to advance under cover of the mangroves, and attack the proas by wading, the tide now being almost at the bottom of the ebb. This had been foreseen by the pirates, however, and as soon as the men emerged from the cover of the mangroves the nearest proa fired her swivel at them, without effect, and all the proas got under way and made sail with great dexterity. The Marines waded out breast-deep to fire on them, but no hits were observed; indeed, breast-deep in surging water is not the best position for using a weapon of precision, far less a smooth-bore flint-lock musket. However, the attack had the desired effect of driving the pirates away completely, for they were never seen again, although no doubt they would later return to break up the remains of the wreck.

The vessel turned out to be the TERNATE, one of the Honourable Company's armed ships, Captain Ellis, which had been despatched by Lord Amherst the day he arrived at Batavia. It was evening before the captain was able to get ashore, and he has recorded the scene within the stockade: the shelters, covered with sailcloth or with palm-leaves; the wild appearance of the men, unshaven and ragged, with their rough pikes and cutlasses in their hands, glinting in the firelight; and the perfect discipline with which they fell into their divisions on the word of command.

On arrival at Batavia, Lord Amherst chartered the Company's ship CAESAR to take the whole party to England, and after a prosperous voyage, touching at Cape Town, the ship reached St Helena on the 27th June 1817. Napoleon received the party with great courtesy, and when Lord Amherst presented Captain Maxwell, the Exile, bowing with great dignity, said (with his extraordinary memory) that the name was known to him, from the Adriatic. 'Your government must not blame you for the loss of the ALCESTE, for you have taken one of my frigates.' When they arrived in England, Captain Maxwell stood his court martial for the loss of the ALCESTE, and was honourably acquitted in the most gratifying terms, and shortly afterwards he was knighted. On the whole, Sir Murray Maxwell had no cause to regret his voyage to China and his shipwreck; he had demonstrated once more to the world the qualities of a British crew, well commanded, in striking contrast to the *Medusa* disaster the year before; he had had a rollicking adventure; and he had not lost a man.

Glossary

All terms are defined in the sense they bore during the period of the book.

ABACK: a sail is aback when the wind is pressing it against the mast.

ABOUT: to go about is to change course, especially when tacking.

ANCHOR: bower, those stowed nearest the head; best bower, then on the starboard, small bower on larboard; both same size. Sheet anchors, those stowed aft of the bowers. Stream anchor, a smaller size. Kedge anchor, usually with more than two flukes, used for dragging-off a grounded vessel.

BACK: a wind backs if its direction changes counter-clockwise.

BEATING: proceeding to windward in a series of zig-zags; tacking.

BRACES: ropes fastened to the yardarms, for swinging them around.

BROACH-TO: to lose steerage way and lie helpless parallel to the troughs of the waves.

CAT-HEAD: a short strong beam projecting from the side of the forecastle, to which an anchor is made fast.

CLEW: the lower corner of a square-sail, or aft corner of a fore-and-aft.

CLEW-EARRING: the loop of rope projecting from the clew of a sail, by which it is made fast to the yard.

CLOSE-HAULED: sailing as near to the wind as possible.

CRANK: unstable, liable to capsize.

DRIVER, or spanker; the largest fore-and-aft sail on a full-rigged ship, spread by boom and gaff from the mizzen mast.

FISH: to repair a mast or spar by lashing small timber around it.

HEAVE-TO: to set one or more sails aback, so as to take the way off the ship.

KNOT: a denomination of speed, signifying one nautical mile per hour.

LATEEN: a large triangular sail set on a sloping yard.

LARGE: a large wind is a favourable one, abaft the beam.

RAKE: in gunnery, to sweep the whole length of a ship with shot.

SPRING: to anchor on a spring, a rope is passed out of a stern-port, brought forward and made fast to the anchor-ring before letting go; after the anchor is fast in the ground, hauling or slackening this rope swings the ship as desired.

VEER: a wind veers when its direction changes clockwise.

WAY: a ship is under way when it is moving through the water under control.

WEIGH: to heave up the anchors.

WEAR: when a ship, having been sailing close-hauled, causes the bow to turn away from the wind so as to sail more large, she is said to wear.

Notes on the plates

Plate 1 This splendid painting by Collis is accurate in every detail. The INDEFATIGABLE, crossing the stern of the *Droits de l'Homme*, has backed her main topsail to stop her in that favourable position. The *Droits de l'Homme* is running with the wind under all possible sail in such a tempest, and is taking in one of her jibs, to ease the fore topmast, which was shortly to come down. The AMAZON is coming up under such a press of sail which shows zeal to get into the fight rather than prudence. See page 24 et seq.

Plate 2 A spirited drawing of the chief French success of the wars. The corvette *Baionnaise* has rammed the frigate AMBUSCADE, carrying away her mizzen mast, and the French are boarding and capturing the much larger and more powerful British ship. See page 62 et seq.

Plate 3 The SAN FIORENZO engaging the *Piémontaise* off Cape Comorin, in defence of three East India ships. This engagement is not narrated in the text, being a usual policing job for the frigates, but was a tough one; after a running fight of three days the French ship surrendered. This fine oil painting by Pocock is most accurate, except of course that all the ships are 'closed up' to make the picture.

Plate 4 The FISGARD engaging the *Immortalité*. See page 77 et seq.

Plate 5 Cutting out the *Hermione* from the fortified harbour of Puerto-Caballo in the Caribbean, by the boats of the SURPRISE, seen in the distance. This magnificent painting by Pocock is correct in every detail. Some of the boarding party can be seen aloft making sail while the battle rages furiously on the decks. See page 38 et seq.

Plate 6 SYBILLE and *Forte*. The end of the battle, as the last mast of the *Forte* comes down. See page 57 et seq.

Plate 7 Basque Roads. The IMPERIEUSE leading in the lighter vessels to attack the stranded French ships, which were, of course, not so crowded together as shown. The wreck of the *Jean Bart* is seen in the left foreground; she had stranded a month before while entering the anchorage. See page 100.

Plate 8 Basque Roads. The IMPERIEUSE, 38 guns, attacking the *Calcutta*, 50, which was shortly abandoned by her whole crew; for which the captain was afterwards tried and shot. See page 100.

Plate 9 SAN FIORENZO taking possession of the *Piémontaise*. See plate 3.

Plate 10 ALCESTE and ACTIVE capturing the *Pomone*, off Ancona. The ALCESTE engaged first, was damaged and had to turn away for repair, when the ACTIVE came up to her support. See page 152 and page 161.

Plate 11 The *Constitution* escaping from a powerful British squadron by towing and kedging during a calm. This American drawing is accurate as far as the *Constitution* is concerned, but is by no means so with the British frigates, especially the GUERRIERE. A month later the *Constitution* met the GUERRIERE alone and destroyed her. See page 128.

Plate 12 The GUERRIERE captured by the *Constitution*. She was so much wrecked that she was burned. See page 128 et seq.

Plate 13 The MACEDONIAN captured by the *United States*. Remarkably accurate depiction of the state of the MACEDONIAN just before surrender. See page 130 et seq.

Plate 14 The *Constitution* capturing the JAVA off Salvador, Brazil. The JAVA was shot to pieces and had to be burned, while the *Constitution* had to return home for repairs. See page 133 et seq.

Plate 15 The *Chesapeake* boarded by the crew of the SHANNON. This was probably the last time an important ship was carried by the cutlass. See page 140 et seq.

Plate 16 The *Essex*, left, engaged by the PHOEBE (centre) and the CHERUB, off Valparaiso. It is hard to say what part of the action this is intended to show; the *Essex* lost her main topmast in a squall before the action commenced. By the American artist Corne, who also did the engraving reproduced in Plate 11. See page 149 et seq.

Jacket illustration Squadron off Lissa. The key manœuvre which resulted eventually in Captain Hoste's amazing victory against odds of more than two to one. See page 115 et seq.

APPENDIX 2

Tonnage

Tonnage has always been a calculation, and varies very widely according to the factors used. It has been said to have been originally based on the number of tuns of wine which could be stowed, but there are doubts on this theory. At the period covered by this book, tonnage was calculated thus:

Length × breadth × ½ breadth, divided by 94.

In Britain, the measure was taken (in feet) from the outside of the stem to the outside of the sternpost, and for the breadth over the outside of the planking. In America, the length was measured inside the posts, and the breadth over the framing excluding the planking; and the divisor was 95. Thus when the *President* was captured and brought into Portsmouth, it was found that whereas by American measure she was 1,444 tons, by British measure she was 1,533. This caused a silly outcry that the Americans were trying to deceive the world about the real size of their frigates; but the methods of American surveyors were well known, and any nation could adopt any factors they pleased. The general idea was to arrive at a 'ton' of 100 cubic feet, and the American method was probably more accurate.

At present, there are in Britain four methods of estimating tonnage, which arrive at widely different results; and there are about a dozen more elsewhere. They can't all be right.

TABLES

Table I Comparative strength of the Royal Navy, 1794 with 1814

Table II Comparative strength of frigates, 1794 with 1814

TABLE I

Strength of the Royal Navy, 1794 compared with 1814

Rate	Guns	Average tonnage	1794			1814		
			In full commission	Reserve or repair	Relegated	In full commission	Reserve or repair	Relegated
First 3 decks	100/120	2,500	5	1	none	7	none	2
Second 3 decks	98	2,200	9	7	3	5	3	4
Third 2 decks	64/80	1,750	71	24	22	87	16	80
Fourth 2 decks	50	1,100	8	4	7	8	2	9
Fifth 2 decks	44	900	12	3	3	2	none	1
Fifth Frigates	32/44	900	66	3	4	121	11	45
Sixth Frigates	28	600	22	2	4	none	none	4
Sixth Post-ship	20/24	500	10	2	2	25	4	11
Unrated vessels	4/18	70/450	76	3	7	360	6	46

TABLE II

Comparative force of the frigates of the Royal Navy, 1794 compared with 1814

Rating by long guns	Average tonnage	Main battery (pounders)	1794			1814		
			In full commission	Reserve or repair	Relegated	In full commission	Reserve or repair	Relegated
44	1,400	24	none	none	none	1	none	2
40	1,260	24	none	none	none	5	none	none
40	1,150	18	none	none	none	1	2	none
38	1,050	18	11	none	none	51	6	12
36	950	18	8	none	1	48	3	10
36	930	12	10	none	3	3	none	11
32	900	18	1	none	none	3	none	4
32	750	12	36	3	3	9	none	4
28	600	12	22	2	4	none	none	4

Index

In this index, names of British warships are in SMALL CAPITALS
Names of enemy warships are in *italics*
People, places and topics are in ordinary type
Ranks are those at the time of mention
Abbreviations: Adm–Admiral; Cmdre–Commodore; Cdr–
Commander

The figure in brackets after the name of a ship denotes her
rated number of guns; the number actually carried was usually
greater